Carmen Cadierno, Mabel Soracco & Jon Hird

Inside Out

Student's Book

Level II

MACMILLAN

S1

Me

Them

People are different

Reading

1 Read the following extracts. Which types of texts in the box do they come from? There are two extra types.

> an e-mail to a cyberpal   a horoscope   a novel   a personal page
> a letter to a pen friend   a magazine article   a film review

a

> **HANDSOME MAN**, 30s, friendly and fun-loving, is looking for an attractive woman, preferably blonde and slim for friendship or love.
>
> Please send photo.
> PO Box 4, Kingston.

b

> Ronald Cross is the most attractive character. He's honest, kind, and considerate – the opposite of bossy, competitive Nina Sands, who doesn't trust anybody, not even herself. Both characters are superbly played by two of the most talented actors in British cinema these days. Do not miss this first-class film version of one of the most popular novels of the last decade.

c

> I'm quite an adventurous person. I love risk sports, so I've tried quite a few: skydiving, windsurfing, mountain climbing … I'm not interested in quiet weekends at home listening to music or playing video games. What about you? How do you like to spend your free time? E-mail me asap.

d

> People who are born under Cancer are loyal to their friends and very sensitive. They are also sensible – they always make the right decision. They enjoy family life and looking after their home. They can also be moody, however. The men tend to be stocky, and the women are often rather plump. Their best choice of a career is probably teaching, nursing or social work.

2 Match the photos (*1–4*) to the texts (*a–d*) in 1. What helped you do the matching?

3 Underline the adjectives describing people in the texts above. Then group them into the following categories: a) physical appearance; b) personality. How many positive adjectives have you found in each category?

4 Look again at the two lists of adjectives you found in 3. Do any of the adjectives apply to you? Compare with a partner.

5 Choose either three people you know or three famous people. Describe their physical appearance and personality to your partner. Use the adjectives from the lists in 3 and /or other adjectives you know.

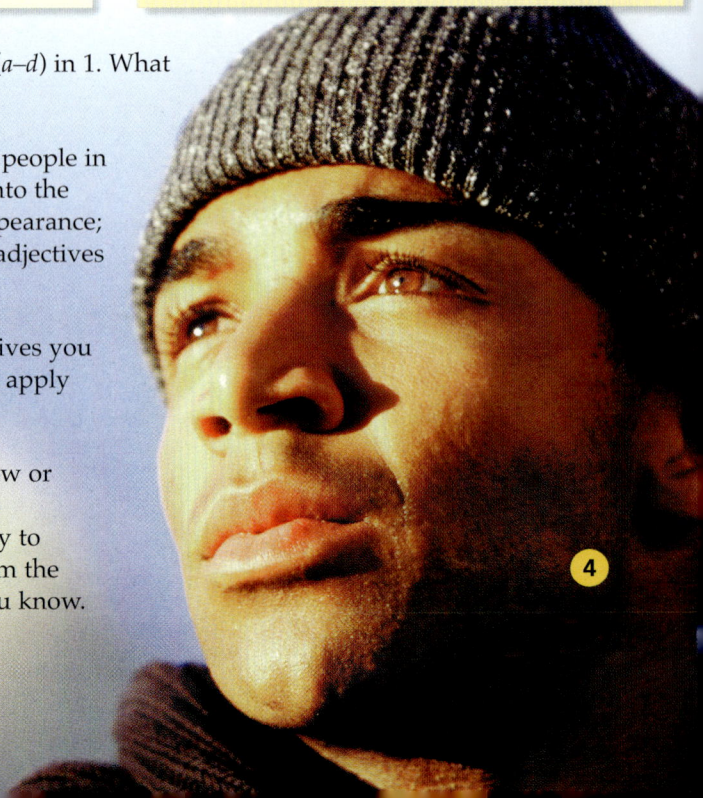

My first home

1 Claire Grogan, who presents a TV programme about films for Sky Premier, tells us about her first home. Read the text and answer the questions below.

'(1) In 1983 I bought a flat with my best friend, Elizanne. It was a first-floor flat in Lansdowne Crescent (2) in Glasgow. We paid (3) £23,000, which was quite a lot at the time. But the flat was beautiful.

The flat had (4) two bedrooms and a large reception room, with two wonderful floor-to-ceiling windows. The kitchen was not a bad size, with a nice breakfast bar. The only problem was (5) the bathroom: it had no window and was really like a large cupboard.

Elizanne worked for her family's curtain company, so we had the most incredible curtains in (6) lilac and pink at a very nice price. My bedroom was pink with a 1980s bedroom suite. The bed, the chest of drawers and the wardrobe were all black and white.

Living on our own in our early twenties made us feel liberated. We really grew up in the first couple of years living there together because we had the responsibility of paying our own mortgage and bills.

After living in the flat for six years, I moved (7) to London because my boyfriend lived there and I was working in television and started doing theatre. Elizanne stayed at Lansdowne Crescent for a while, but in 1990 we decided (8) to sell the flat. We sold it for £69,000.'

(Adapted from *The Daily Telegraph*, Saturday 2ⁿᵈ February 2002)

a) How many rooms did the flat have?
b) How did they feel living on their own?
c) How long did they have the flat?
d) What was the difference between the price of the flat in 1983 and 1990?

2 Find the words or phrases in the text that could replace the underlined words and phrases below.

a) The flat had large windows.
b) The size of the kitchen was all right.
c) The bathroom was too small.
d) The curtains were not expensive.
e) We became more adult.
f) We had the responsibility of paying back the money we borrowed to buy the house.

3 Work with a partner. Look at the highlighted words in the text. Ask each other the questions that would give you those answers.

For example: *1 When did they buy the flat?*

Speaking Work with your partner and ask each other questions about the place where you live.

For example:

- Do you live in a flat or a house? Where is it located? What's it like? How many rooms has it got?
- How long have you lived there?
- Do you live on your own or do you share it with other people?
- How do you feel about your home?

Writing Write a description of your home in about 100 words. Organise your description into 2 paragraphs:

Paragraph 1 Factual information
Paragraph 2 Your feelings

Classroom language

What do you say when you want ...

a) to know the meaning of a word in English?
b) to know how to say a word in English?
c) to write a word and don't know the spelling?
d) to borrow a pen?
e) to ask somebody to repeat something?
f) to ask for a handout?

Secrets

Work with a partner. Discuss the following questions.

- How good are you at keeping secrets?
- What kinds of things do people usually keep secret? What about you?

Reading & listening

1 ☐ 04 Read and listen to Kate's story. Then answer the questions below.

The photo album

AFTER THE FUNERAL my husband took the children home, and I went back to my parents' house – the house I grew up in. I moved about, from room to room, looking at the old familiar things, thinking, remembering, reliving the past. The house had so many memories of our life together as a family: my father and my mother, Sarah and me.

There was so much to do. Insurance, bank accounts … and the house. I'd have to sell it. At least there wouldn't be too much to clear out: my father hated mess. 'If in doubt, throw it out.' I had heard him say those words a thousand times.

I started in the attic, which almost made me cry. It was so much like him. It was immaculately clean, and everything was organised in boxes with labels: 'Bank statements', 'Winter clothes', 'Books 1: philosophy' …

While I was moving a large suitcase labelled 'Exam papers', I was surprised to find a small box with no label at all. It was about thirty centimetres square, covered in brown leather and locked. There was no key. Perhaps I shouldn't open it. Too private, maybe. But what difference could it make now? I took a metal ruler from a box of office equipment, and put some pressure under the lid, until finally it opened. Inside there was a photo album. Excited, but a little worried for some reason, I opened the album.

The album was full of normal family photos – a day by the sea, cricket in the garden, a new car. My father was in several of the photos, smiling for the camera. But I wasn't there, and neither was my sister. Instead there were two little boys. The garden wasn't our garden. And the woman with my father in the new car wasn't my mother. She was someone I had never seen before …

a) Whose funeral did Kate attend?
b) What was Kate going to do with her parents' house?
c) Why was the attic like her father?
d) Why didn't Kate want to open the box at first?
e) What did Kate find inside the box?
f) What was her father's secret?

2 Work with a partner. Discuss these questions.

a) In your opinion, how did Kate feel after she found the photo album and discovered her father's secret?
b) Do you think Kate's mother knew this secret?
c) What do you think Kate will do next?

Language awareness

Adjectives ending in -ing/-ed

1 Look at the two cartoons and write the correct adjectives: *bored* or *boring*; *excited* or *exciting*.

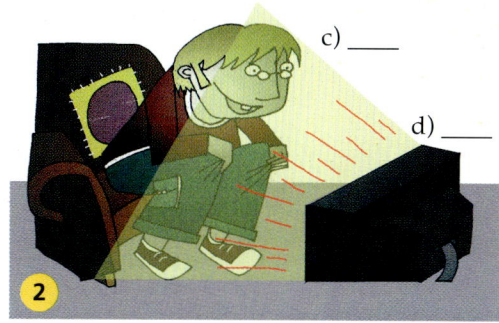

a) ____ b) ____ c) ____ d) ____

2 Underline the correct alternatives.

a) When Kate went up to the attic, she felt **depressed/depressing**.
b) It was **tired/tiring** for Kate to organise her father's papers.
c) The photos in the album were very **surprised/surprising**.
d) Kate was **shocked/shocking** when she looked at the photos.
e) She felt **disappointed/disappointing** that her father had never mentioned his other family.
f) After some time Kate thought it would be **interested/interesting** to find out more about her father's other family.

3 Look back at the sentences in 2. Then complete the following statements with *-ing* or *-ed*.

a) The ____ forms are used to say how someone feels.
b) The ____ forms are used to describe the people or things that cause that feeling.

4 Discuss how these adjectives are translated into Spanish.

Pronunciation: the -ed ending

1 Work with a partner. Underline the words in which the ending *-ed* is pronounced /ɪd/.

depressed	lived	opened	decided	looked	hated	started	organised	needed
surprised	wanted	interested	locked	disappointed	enjoyed	shocked	excited	

2 ▭ 05 Listen and check your answers.

3 What do all the /ɪd/ words have in common? Can you add more examples? How are the other endings pronounced?

Speaking

Think of a secret (real or invented). Then in groups of three find out each person's secret by asking some or all of the questions below. Try to use some of the adjectives from the *Language awareness* section in your answers.

- Was it your secret?
- Whose secret was it?
- How old were you?
- How did you find out?
- How did you feel? Why?

- How long did you keep it a secret?
- Did you tell anybody? Why / Why not?
- Who did you tell?
- What happened then?

Writing

Now choose one of the group's secrets and write 100–120 words about it. Use the questions in the speaking activity to organise your ideas. When you finish, read your piece of writing through and check your grammar and spelling.

S4 Sport

Fit

Lexis: sports clothes & equipment

1 Match the words in the box with the pictures.

| vest   tracksuit   racket   net   swimsuit   skis   trainers   goal   helmet   shorts |

a b c d e f g h i j

Comparatives

Language reference p27

2 Look at the photos of sportspeople from the past and write about how sports clothes and equipment have changed. Make comparisons using the adjectives in the box.

| light/heavy   tight/loose   colourful   fashionable   small/big |
| short/long   expensive/cheap   good/bad |

1 2 3

For example: *Tennis rackets were heavier then. They are lighter now.*

3 Work with a partner. Talk about other sports clothes and equipment. How have they changed in the last 30 years?

For example: *Tracksuits were tighter in the 1970s. They are looser now.*

4 Match the items in 1 with the sports they are used in.

| athletics   football   motor racing   skiing   swimming   tennis   volleyball |

Speaking

Work with a partner. Think about the sports in 4 and answer the following questions.

a) Which are team sports and which are played individually?
b) In which of the sports do you: (1) throw the ball; (2) hit the ball; (3) catch the ball; (4) kick the ball?
c) Which sport attracts the biggest crowds?
d) In your opinion which is the most dangerous of the sports?
e) Which sport would you do for pleasure?
f) Which sport would you never do?

Sports quiz

1 Test your sporting knowledge. Choose the correct answer for each sentence in the sports quiz below. Then check your answers below.

1 In the 14th century in **Peru / Mexico / Brazil** the Aztecs played tlachtli, a religious ball game in which the players hit a rubber ball with the elbows, knees and hips.

2 The first football World Cup was held in Uruguay in **1930 / 1940 / 1950**.

3 The first Olympic Games were held in Olympia, **Italy / Turkey / Greece**, in approximately 776 BC.

4 The game of **football / volleyball / rugby** was born in 1823 when William Webb Ellis caught the ball with his two hands and ran with it rather than kicking it.

5 Ben Johnson was probably the most famous Olympic **hurdler / sprinter / decathlete** to be disqualified for testing positive for taking steroids at the Seoul games in 1988.

6 When British explorer **David Livingstone / Sir Francis Drake / James Cook** arrived in Tahiti in the 1770s, surfing was the most popular sport on the island. Later on it was prohibited by missionaries, because they said it was immoral.

7 Basketball was started in Massachusetts, USA in 1891, when Dr James Naismith used two **waste paper / peach / fishing** baskets as goals.

8 In 1960 Rome was the venue of the first Olympic Games for **child / women / disabled** athletes.

9 The marathon race originated in 490 BC when Greek messenger Philippides ran **22 / 32 / 42** kilometres to break the news of the Athenian victory over the Persians in the battle of Marathon.

10 The longest boxing match lasted **5 / 7 / 9** hours 19 minutes. It took place in New Orleans, USA in 1893, between Andy Bowen and Jack Burke, and it ended in a draw after 110 rounds.

2 Work with a partner. Ask and answer these questions about the quiz. Do you agree with your partner?

- Which was the easiest answer to choose? Which was the most difficult?
- Which gave the most surprising information?
- How many answers did you know?
- How many were you able to guess?

Classroom language

1 ▭ 06 Listen to seven short dialogues (1–7) and match them with the situations (a–d) below.

a) You're not sure how to do an activity.
b) You are starting an activity.
c) You think you've finished an activity.
d) You are commenting on an activity.

2 Read tapescript 06 on page 188. Listen again and repeat the dialogues with a partner.

1 Mexico 2 1930 3 Greece 4 rugby 5 sprinter 6 James Cook 7 peach 8 disabled 9 42 10 7

Review 1

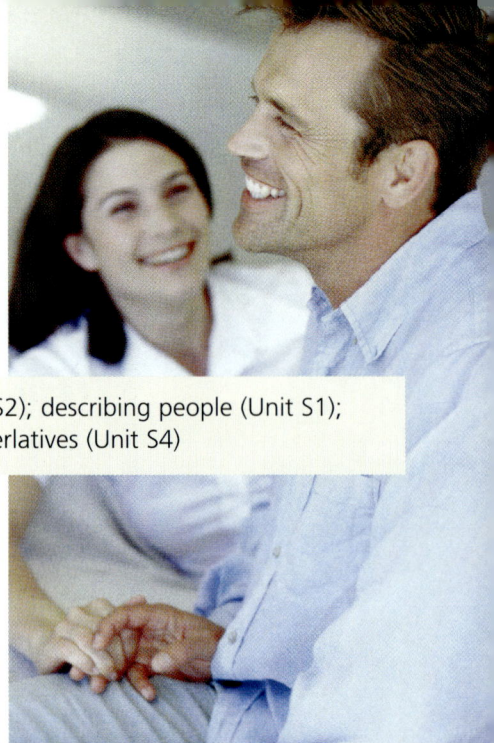

Language reviewed: question formation (Units S1 and S2); describing people (Unit S1); *like / be like / would like* (Unit S2); comparatives and superlatives (Unit S4)

Is it written in the stars?

Reading   Read the article and choose the correct answer.
When Minna was a teenager:

a)   she didn't like Billy.
b)   she didn't know him very well.
c)   she was good friends with Billy.

Minna: I met Billy when I was (1) **three years old and he was four.** We went to the same nursery school and my first memory of Billy is that he was (2) **blonde, thin and very quiet.** He had a pet mouse called Peter which (3) **escaped every day.** He really cared for that mouse. We met again when I was fifteen and Billy was sixteen. He was (4) **outside our local train station** with a group of friends. We started going out with friends, but I never thought he liked me. We shared many interests, such as (5) **playing sport, photography and bird watching!** (6) **We were close** friends but, as I said before, we went out with other people.

Then (7) **he went travelling to Australia and I went to university.** When he came back, we went out together, but I saw him as a friend only – until something suddenly changed. (8) **He gave me a different look** and I realised I was falling in love with him. As soon as I kissed him I knew it was right. It's extraordinary that you could meet the love of your life when you're three.

Billy: One of my first memories of Minna is feeding the tadpoles together at nursery. She was plump and had lots of dark hair. A couple of years later I saw her at a fancy dress party. I couldn't talk to her (9) **because I was so shy and she was talking to all the other children.** When I met Minna again at sixteen I never thought I had a chance as all the boys liked her. She was the prettiest girl in the group and was good fun but she was also great to talk to about your problems. (10) **I got off the bus early** on my way home from school to see her at the train station, then walked miles home. In our twenties that dynamic suddenly changed. We've been together since then.

Questions   Read the article again and write the questions for the highlighted words.

For example: *1 How old were Minna and Billy when they first met?*

**Comparatives
& superlatives**   **1**   Match the adjectives in the box to: a) Minna; b) Billy; c) both Minna and Billy.

> shy   attractive   friendly   fun-loving   adventurous   popular
> quiet   beautiful   kind   sensitive   active   blonde   thin   plump   dark

2   Use the adjectives in brackets to complete this paragraph. Use the comparative and superlative forms of the adjectives.

Minna was the (1) ____ (pretty) girl in the group. Minna was (2) ____ (popular) than Billy. She was also (3) ____ (friendly) and (4) ____ (fun-loving) than Billy. He was (5) ____ (shy) and (6) ____ (quiet) than her.

Work with a partner and discuss the following.

• Do you think it was 'written in the stars' for Minna and Billy? Why / Why not?
• Do you know or have you heard of any other similar cases?
• Do you think it was or it will be 'written in the stars' for you?

like / be like / would like

1 Complete these questions with the correct form of *do*, the verb *be* or *would*. Read the answers to the questions to help you.

a) What ____ Billy like at the age of four? – Thin, blonde and very quiet.
b) What ____ Minna and Billy like doing? – Playing sport, photography and bird watching.
c) What ____ you like to do right now? – Go for a swim.
d) What sports ____ Spaniards like most? – Football and motor racing.
e) What ____ your classmates like? – Young, handsome and good fun!
f) What kind of music ____ young people like? – Jungle and techno.
g) What ____ you like for breakfast tomorrow? – Some toast and a coffee.
h) What ____ you and your friends like doing at weekends? – Going to a disco or to a beach party in the summer.
i) What ____ your best friend's husband like? – Well, he's not terribly attractive, but he's very nice and friendly.
j) What ____ the weather like in your city in summer? – Hot and humid.

2 Now translate the first five questions in 1 into Spanish and discuss them with your teacher and classmates.

Pronunciation: the *-ed* ending

1 Read the text below and:

a) <u>underline</u> all the verbs.
b) (circle) the *-ed* endings pronounced /ɪd/.

2 📼 07 Listen and check your answers.

3 Practise reading the text, paying special attention to the pronunciation of *-ed*.

> *As soon as he arrived home, Inspector Cruise walked to the phone, dialled a secret number and waited. When nobody answered at the other end, he decided to call the police station instead. An angry man's voice shouted 'Who is it?'. The inspector laughed. His men never sounded very happy when they were at work.*

Writing Describe a city or a place that is special to you. Remember to use some of the adjectives in Unit S2. You can also use tapescript 03 on page 188 as a model. Write about 100–120 words.

Speaking Interview your classmates. Choose two of the following topics and prepare 5 or 6 questions to ask different classmates.

- Their favourite celebrity (a sportsperson, actor, musician, leader, politician, etc). Ask about his/her looks, personality, family background, job and any other personal information. (Unit S1)
- The place where they live. Ask about how they feel about living there and what they like and dislike about it. (Unit S2)
- Their flat/house. Ask what it is like and any changes they would like to make. (Unit S2)
- An important event in the past. Ask them what it was and why it was important. (Unit S3)
- Their favourite sport. Ask them which sports they like doing and which sports they like watching. (Unit S4)
- Learning English. Ask when and why they started to learn English and what they think about their progress now.

S6 Souvenirs

Work with a partner. Discuss the following questions.

- How often do you go to museums?
- When was the last time you visited one?
- Did you buy a souvenir? What was it?

Reading & listening

1 Look at this map of central London showing where the most famous museums and galleries are situated. Answer the questions.

a) Which of these places have you heard of?
b) Which of these places have you visited?
c) Which would you most like to visit? Why?

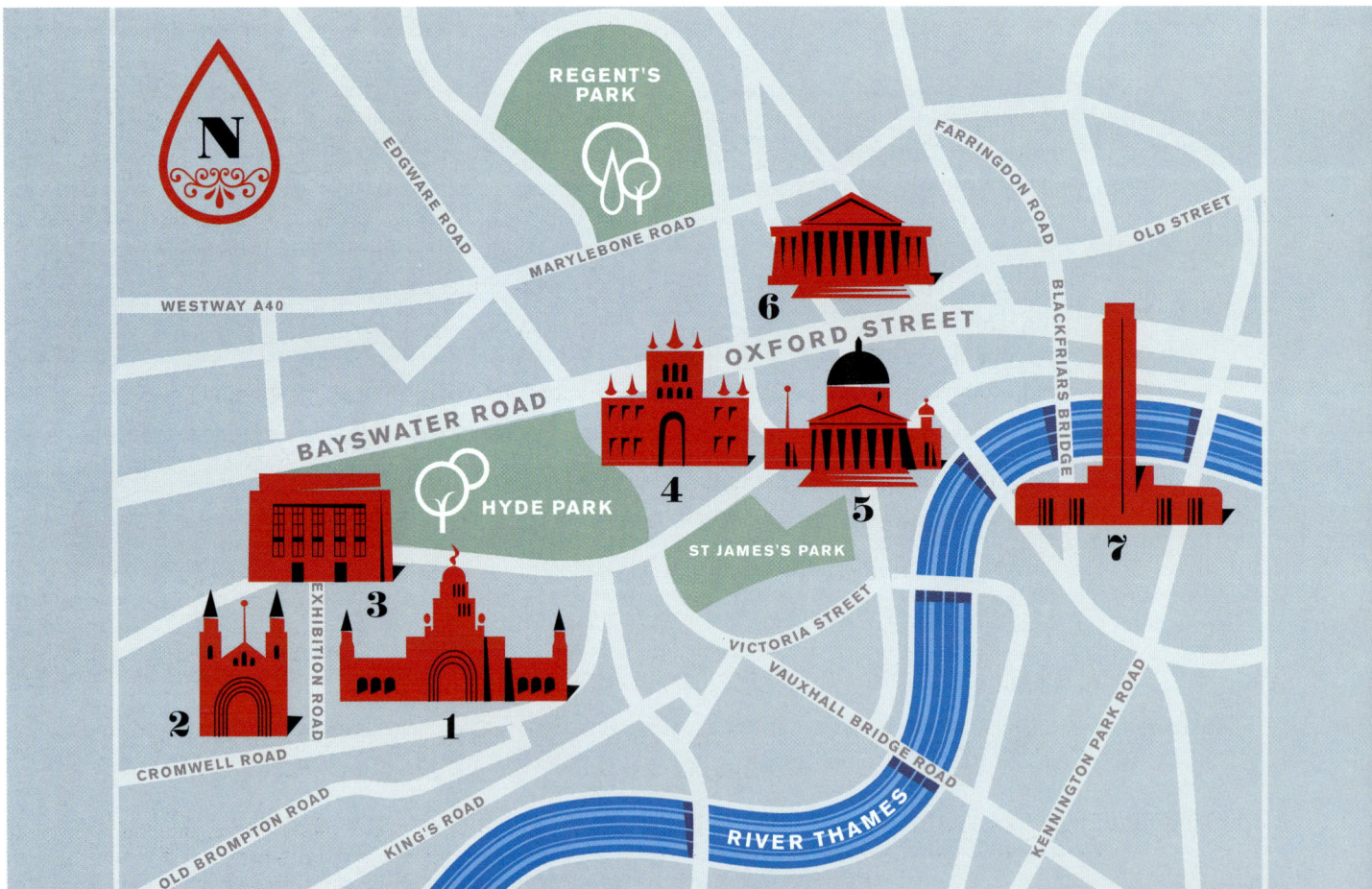

1 The Victoria & Albert Museum
The world's finest collection of decorative arts. The permanent collections include fashion and textiles, jewellery, sculptures, photographs and paintings.

2 The Natural History Museum
Marvels of the natural world from dinosaurs and insects to geology and future Earth.

3 The Science Museum
Objects from every area of science and technology, including space travel, telecommunications, computing, chemistry, photography, medicine and more!

4 The Royal Academy of Arts
Holds exhibitions of works by Gainsborough, Turner, Constable and other famous English painters from the 18th century through to the present day.

5 The National Gallery
One of the world's greatest collections of European art including works by Raphael, Rembrandt, Velázquez, Goya, Rubens, Da Vinci and Monet.

6 The British Museum
The world's first public museum containing over four million artefacts from the ancient world through to the present day.

7 Tate Modern
The most exciting collection of modern and contemporary art in Britain, including paintings, sculpture and installations.

2 🔲 **08** Read and listen to the text. Which of the places on the map is **not** mentioned?

Pay and display

ANDY WARHOL once said that department stores were like museums. Today, large museums and art galleries are like department stores. Museum and art gallery shops are more than just fun shopping, they're an integral part of the 'museum experience'. Visitors like buying things which remind them of their visit.

● According to Damien Whitmore at the Victoria and Albert Museum: 'Exhibition shops allow you to take a bit of the museum home with you – people always want a souvenir from their visit. For our current exhibition, *Tiaras*, we've stocked the shop with … beautiful tiaras costing from £150 up to £1,425.' The V&A range also includes stationery, wallpaper and carpets.

● Similarly Tate Modern has collaborated with famous jewellers and designers to produce a permanent range of articles for its shop. And when its exhibition, *Surrealism: Desire Unbound* opened, top designers Agent Provocateur created a range of lingerie for the show and exclusive cosmetics company MAC produced a make-up set. Since the Warhol retrospective opened in February, the shop has sold more than 4,000 Warhol mugs.

● The Natural History Museum has collaborated with contemporary designers to produce a surprising variety of items made from recycled materials. It includes coasters made from coffee cups, yoghurt pots and juice cartons for £1.99.

● The British Museum includes fashionable and well-priced jewellery of the most popular objects in its collection.

● When *Rembrandt's Women* was showing at the Royal Academy, the shop produced a wide variety of jewellery similar to the jewellery the women wear in the paintings.

● Similarly the National Gallery offers replica slippers and scarves as worn in some of its famous paintings.

It used to be hard to find anything to spend money on in museum shops. Now it can be difficult to leave empty-handed.

(Adapted from *The Times*, Saturday 13th April 2002)

3 Read the text again more carefully and answer the questions.

a) Why are museums and art galleries like department stores?
b) What do visitors like buying?
c) Why can it be difficult now to leave a museum or a gallery empty-handed?

Lexis: souvenirs

1 Work with a partner. Put the words in the box into the following categories. Use a dictionary to check the meaning of the words you don't know.

| carpets   coasters   jewellery   lingerie   make-up   mugs scarves |
| slippers   stationery   tiaras   wallpaper |

Accessories: ____   Cosmetics: ____   Household items: ____
Clothing/shoes: ____   Equipment used for writing: ____

2 Can you remember in which museums or galleries you can buy the articles in 1? Write the articles under the appropriate headings. Check the text again if you need to.

Victoria & Albert	Natural History	Royal Academy	National Gallery	British Museum	Tate Modern

Speaking

1 Tell your partner which of the items above you would like to buy as a present for your family or friends and why. Which one would you get for yourself? Explain why.

2 Work with another partner and discuss the following questions.

● How do the Spanish museum shops you know compare with the ones mentioned in the text? Do they sell the same kinds of products?
● What do you think about this type of museum shop?
● When you go to a museum what part of the visit do you enjoy most?
● Why do people go to museums?

Work

Lexis: *work* or *job*?

1 What is the difference between *work* and *job*? Complete the following sentences with the appropriate form of *work* or *job*.

a) I can't go to the cinema this weekend – I've got a lot of ____ to do.
b) I'm applying for the ____ advertised in your magazine.
c) Ann ____ in the same office as me.
d) He's had three different ____ this year already.
e) What time do you finish ____?
f) I got my first ____ when I was seventeen.

2 Look at the sentences in 1 again and then complete the table with *work* or *job*.

Countable noun, singular	Countable noun, plural	Uncountable noun	Verb
job			

Dream jobs

Listening

1 🔲 09 Listen to the answers these four people gave to the same question. What was the question they were asked?

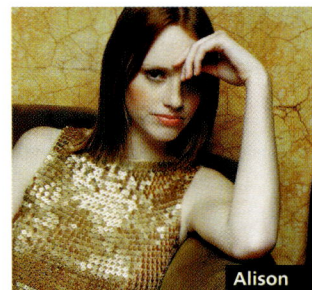
Alison

2 Listen again and answer these questions.

a) What are the jobs mentioned?
b) What are the speakers' present jobs?
c) Who is doing the job that he/she always wanted to do?

3 Ask your partner the same question as the speakers were asked in the recording.

Ben

4 Which of the jobs mentioned in the recording would be best for you? Which would be worst for you? Why? Compare with a partner.

Language awareness

Past simple & present perfect

1 Look at tapescript 09 for Alison on page 188 and copy the past simple verb phrases in the left-hand column and the present perfect ones in the right-hand column below.

I was	I've always enjoyed

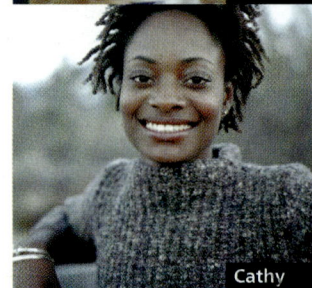
Cathy

2 Label the two columns with these headings: *Finished* and *Unfinished (continuing up to now)*.

3 Add more present perfect verb phrases from tapescript 09.

4 Write a short paragraph about yourself using tapescript 09 as a model.

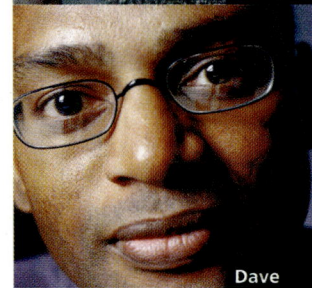
Dave

Curriculum vitae (CV)

Discussion   Work with a partner. Discuss the following questions.

- Why do people write CVs?
- What kind of information is given in a CV?
- Have you ever written your CV? Why / Why not?

Reading   **1**   Read the CV below. What job do you think Orla is applying for?

2   Put these headings (*A–F*) in the correct places (*1–6*) on the CV.

A Education	C Personal details	E Referees
B Profile	D Work experience	F Interests

CURRICULUM VITAE

1 _____

NAME:	Orla McCarthy
ADDRESS:	5 Oak Park Street, London W12 6BBN England
DATE OF BIRTH:	12.12.1973
TELEPHONE:	(00 44) (0)2088 406043 Mobile: 0744 432691
E-MAIL:	o.mccarthy@notmail.com
NATIONALITY:	Irish

2 _____

Outgoing, reliable and enthusiastic, I work well on my own and as part of a team. I adapt quickly to new situations and am willing to take risks to get a good story. However, I am sensible and stay calm in difficult situations. I have an excellent knowledge of French.

3 _____

1994–1995	BBC Graduate training programme (TV journalism), London
1991–1994	Bachelor of Arts degree in English and History, University College, Dublin
1984–1991	Loretto Secondary School, Dublin

4 _____

2001 to present	BBC TV Middle East correspondent (Cairo)
2000–2001	BBC TV Junior correspondent in Afghanistan
1998–2000	BBC World Service TV, Eastern Desk
1996–1998	TV reporter for BBC Oxford

5 _____

Travel, politics, languages, culture, Irish music, tennis

6 _____

PROFESSIONAL:	Ms F Peterson, BBC World Service, London WC2B 4PH
PERSONAL:	Dr JP O'Sullivan, 8 Saval Park Road, Dublin 4

Writing   **1**   Write your own CV or profile (real or invented) following the model above. Decide which job you are applying for before you start.

2   Now read other students' CVs or profiles. Can you guess the job they are applying for?

FALSE FRIENDS

Match the underlined words with their English translations. In some cases more than one answer is possible.

1 Qué harás cuando acabes la <u>carrera</u>?	a) college	e) studies
2 Lo primero es <u>solicitar</u> un trabajo.	b) solicit	f) talk
3 El <u>colegio</u> de los niños está cerca de casa.	c) conference	g) career
4 La <u>conferencia</u> que dio el escritor invitado fue muy interesante.	d) apply for	h) school

Spend

Work with a partner. Discuss the questions.

- How much of your money do you spend? How much of your money do you save?
- What do you spend your money on?
- Why do so many people like to go shopping during sales? What about you?
- Imagine you find something that is a bargain but you don't need it. What do you do?

How to spend money

Listening

1 Anna Lewis is a successful 35-year-old restaurant owner in London. Read the questions a radio reporter asked Anna about how she spends her money. Use the words in the box to try to predict as many of her answers as you can.

Anna

▶ earns £35,000 a year.

▶ saves £1,000 a year.

▶ gives £500 a year to charity.

spending money (n): money you spend on things you want, not on food and bills

car boot sale: a market where people sell things they don't want from the back of their car

outing (n): a short journey that you take for enjoyment

| her mobile phone   a bikini   about £300   a van (£180)   Portugal (£1,000) |
| a PlayStation   nothing   cash   her daughter |

a) Where did you go on your last holiday and how much did it cost?
b) What's your worst-ever buy?
c) What's your best bargain?
d) Are you a credit card person or a cash person?
e) What do you feel you waste your money on?
f) How much do you spend on lunch each week?
g) Where does most of your money go?
h) How much do you spend on clothes?
i) What's the most expensive present you've ever bought someone?

2 🔲 10 Listen and check your answers. Write down one extra detail for each question.

Speaking

Choose five or six questions from the previous section and interview three classmates. Do you spend your money the same way? Is there anything that surprises you in the way they spend their money?

Lexis: easily confused words

1 Work with a partner. Choose the correct alternative in each sentence.

a) Anna **passes/spends** a lot of money on shoes.
b) Time **passed/spent**, but there was no news of the lost child.
c) I'm going to **pass/spend** the weekend in the country.
d) Anna feels she **loses/wastes** her money on her mobile phone.
e) You're **losing/wasting** your time. You'll never convince him.
f) When the business collapsed, we **lost/wasted** all our money.
g) How much does a restaurant owner **earn/win**?
h) When he goes to the casino, he always **earns/wins**. He's a lucky man.
i) If I ever **earn/win** the lottery, I'll give up my job!

2 Work with a partner. Complete the sentences with *pass* or *spend*, *lose* or *waste*, and *earn* or *win*.

pass **or** *spend*
a) When you ____ time or money you are normally doing it because you have decided to.
b) Time always ____.

lose **or** *waste*
a) If you ____ time or money, you don't know where it's gone.
b) If you ____ time or money, you know where it's gone and you are unhappy about it.

earn **or** *win*
a) To ____ money, you usually need to be lucky.
b) To ____ money, you need to have a job.

3 Read the letter and circle the correct verbs.

Dear Liz

How are you doing? Sorry I haven't been in touch for so long. I got your e-mail a couple of weeks ago, but the days seem to (1) **pass/spend** so quickly – especially when you've got teenage children! Anyway, I thought I'd write a letter instead of an e-mail for a change.

We're all fine. Tom is (2) **passing/spending** the summer holiday working in a sports shop in town. He says he wants to (3) **earn/win** some money for university next year – but I know he'll (4) **lose/waste** it all on computer games, as usual! Boys – they're all the same.

Clara is so different from Tom. She saves everything she (5) **earns/wins** from her babysitting and never (6) **loses/wastes** a penny. She's going to be a rich woman one day!

Oh, and did I tell you about Sara? She (7) **earned/won** £250 in a photography competition. First prize! Rick and I were so proud of her. I think she's going to (8) **pass/spend** the prize money on a digital camera.

Unfortunately, I haven't been so lucky with money lately. Can you imagine, I left my handbag on the train yesterday and (9) **lost/wasted** £50. I went to the lost property office, but I was (10) **losing/wasting** my time. Oh well – it's only money, I suppose. Easy come, easy go, as they say!

Anyway, I've got to stop now. Today is our wedding anniversary, and Rick and I are (11) **passing/spending** the night in a five star hotel!

I'll ring you next week for a proper chat.

Love
Tracy
X X X

Writing

1 Work with a partner. Read Tracy's letter again and underline useful words and phrases for letter writing.

2 Write a letter to a friend telling them how you've spent your time and money recently. Use Tracy's letter as a model. Include the useful words and phrases you underlined in 1.

Competition

Rules

Work with a partner. Discuss the following questions.

- Have you taken part in many competitions?
- What type of competitions were they?
- What did you do to enter?
- Did you win anything?

Reading

1 Read the competition and decide what type of people would enter this competition.

2 Read the competition again and complete the text with the most appropriate modal or phrase from the box.

must	are not allowed	must	are not allowed	don't have to	mustn't	shouldn't	must

WIN £10,000

Do you want to be the star of your own fashion business? Enter this competition with *ELLA* and you could win £10,000. GO FASHION!

Have you got the talent and ideas of Donatella Versace but not her money? Do you dream of having your own boutique, starting a model agency or being a photographer? It's hard to show the world how good you are if you don't have the money but one lucky *ELLA* reader can. Whatever your fashion idea *ELLA* has the answer to your money problems. We'll give you £10,000 to realise your fashion dream.
The winner will receive £10,000 and their idea will be in the summer edition of *ELLA*. Two runners-up will receive £5,000 each.

HOW TO ENTER

To take part, you (1) _____ write a 100-word summary of your idea. We want to know all the details: what you would like to do, how you will make it work, who or what inspires you. Photographers, stylists and designers (2) _____ forget to include recent examples of your work (unfortunately, these cannot be returned). You (3) _____ buy anything. Just send the above, along with the completed coupon/form (opposite) and a passport-sized photograph to this address: *ELLA* Competition, Endeavour House, 299 Shaftesbury Avenue, London WC2H JJG.

TERMS & CONDITIONS

- We will not accept any entries after the closing date.
- All entrants (4) _____ be over 18. Employees of *ELLA* or any other of its agents or any company connected with the competition (5) _____ enter. Neither are any of their relatives or members of their families.
- Readers (6) _____ to enter the competition more than once.
- Winners (7) _____ agree to the publication of their name and photograph in *ELLA*.
- Readers outside the UK or the Republic of Ireland (8) _____ to enter the competition.

Language awareness

Modals of advice, obligation & permission

1 Read your answers to the previous exercise again. Which modals or phrases express the following:

Advice: _____ No obligation: _____

Obligation: _____ Prohibition: _____ and _____

2 Write five sentences about yourself using all the modals and phrases from 1. Then, compare your sentences with your partner's. Are any of your sentences the same?

For example: *I'm not allowed to wear jeans to work.*

Design a competition

Speaking & writing

1 The following competitions appeared on the Internet. What are the subjects/topics of the three competitions advertised?

a)

Nikon

NIKON MICROSCOPY SMALL WORLD COMPETITION

b)

5k

The 5k: an award for excellence in web design and production

c)

Julian Gayarre

The 9th Julian Gayarre International Singing Competition

2 In groups of three or four, create a competition for students of English in EOIs. Here are some ideas:

science, photography, web design, music, general knowledge, an invention, painting, poetry, fitness and strength

3 Decide on the following details:

- The theme of the competition (you can choose either one of the ideas given above or your own – you could always get ideas from the Internet)
- The prize (a car, a holiday, money, something for the home)
- The task (sing a song, take a photograph, write a story / poem / quiz, design a web page / an invention)
- The terms and conditions for entry
- The closing date for entry
- The address to send the entries to

4 Choose a group secretary to write up your competition. Use the fashion competition as a model.

5 Put your competition up on the wall. Look at other groups' competitions. Vote for the one you like most. Why do you like it? Which one would you enter? Explain why. Discuss your choices with the rest of the class.

FALSE FRIENDS

Choose the English word that corresponds to the underlined word in Spanish.

1 Hay que rellenar un formulario para <u>presentarse</u> a una competición.
2 El número de <u>inscripciones</u> es limitado.
3 Enviar el impreso a la <u>dirección</u> que se indica.
4 Los <u>parientes</u> de los empleados ya saben las condiciones.

a) **present/enter**
b) **entries/inscriptions**
c) **direction/address**
d) **parents/relatives**

Developing exam strategies 1

Language reviewed: past simple and past continuous (Unit S3); present perfect and past simple (Unit S7); modals (Unit S9)

In this unit you will be given the chance to develop your exam strategies by:

- practising different skills and exercise types found in English exams
- reflecting on how you did these exercises
- thinking about other ways you could approach them

Grammatical/linguistic competence

1 Read the article and choose the most appropriate verb form.

THE BEST PRESENT

My whole life (1) **is changing / has changed** since Christmas Day when, thanks to the best present I (2) **have ever had / had**, I turned my living room into a pub. The gift in question was a karaoke machine and I (3) **haven't stopped / didn't stop** singing since then. La la laaaa! I (4) **became / have become** so completely obsessed that sometimes I have to sing a song when I am alone in the middle of the day. The phone (5) **is ringing / rings** unanswered, appointments are forgotten: I'm too busy being Edith Piaf, or Judy Garland or … others.

Karaoke is addictive. Even my mother (6) **sang / has sung** an Elvis song in public the last time she came to visit us. Karaoke gets us all in the end.

When I (7) **am / was** at school in the 1970s, we (8) **had to / must** attend chapel every morning. I (9) **love / loved** the hymns, but I couldn't sing them properly. When I (10) **was opening / opened** my mouth my teachers turned around to look at me angrily. Finally, they said, 'For God's sake, stop singing! Just STOP IT.' It took a year before they realised I (11) **didn't do / wasn't doing** it as a joke. I've gone from the type of person who didn't sing a note in public to the type of person who can't stop singing in public. In the process, I (12) **have made / made** some interesting discoveries. One is the fact that I (13) **can / could** sometimes sing men's songs quite well, but only if I'm a little drunk! Still, at least I know I (14) **can't / shouldn't** sing anything very well – not many people are conscious of this. The worst people are the ones who say, 'Oh, I love singing!' and then, they proceed to sing badly for an hour. Interestingly, singing in public is a useful indicator of people's own self-image. Sometimes it's difficult not to laugh. But that's the thing about karaoke – it (15) **is / was** always a laugh. Even if the laugh's on you!

(Adapted from *Nova*, May 2001)

2 Read the grammar exam strategies below. How many of these did you use to do the exercise above?

STRATEGIES

- I looked at the photo and thought about the title to help me understand the text.
- I read the whole text to get the gist / main ideas.
- I didn't stop and worry about words I didn't understand.
- I looked for words referring to the past, present and future to help me to choose the right tense.
- I chose one answer even when I wasn't sure which of the alternatives was correct.
- (add others you used)

3 Work with a partner and compare the strategies you used. What would you do differently next time?

I needed a change

Listening
comprehension

1 🔊 **11** Listen to an interview with Joseph Kome, a footballer who moved from Senegal a year ago to play football in England. Choose the correct answer.

1   As a child …
   a)   he had a favourite English team.
   b)   he didn't have a TV.
   c)   he was only able to watch the goals on TV.

2   He moved to England because …
   a)   he had read about a football trial in the newspaper.
   b)   he wanted a change.
   c)   his club transferred him.

3   When he was offered a contract …
   a)   he discussed it with his agent for a long time.
   b)   he signed for only one season.
   c)   he accepted immediately.

4   At first …
   a)   he wasn't familiar with the English way of playing.
   b)   he found the English game very easy.
   c)   he was too aggressive.

5   He finds …
   a)   life is too quiet in England.
   b)   people are more impatient in his country.
   c)   the cost of living in England isn't very different from in his country.

2 Read the listening exam strategies below. Put each group under the appropriate heading.

Before listening	While listening	After listening

STRATEGIES

A   I went through all the questions and answered the ones I was confident were correct and then looked at all the alternatives for the ones I wasn't sure about.

B   I checked all my answers again and then chose an answer on the ones I wasn't sure about.

C   I took some notes and I checked if the multiple choice answers were in sequence.

D   I read the instructions carefully and <u>underlined</u> key words. I then looked at the photo and read the title.
I read all the multiple choice answers so I knew what I needed to listen for.

3 Work with a partner and compare the strategies you used. What would you do differently next time?

Writing

1 As Joseph Kome is going to visit your town next month, you've been asked to write a short biography of this footballer for the school magazine. Use tapescript 11 on page 189 to help you. Include the following points:

- how long he has played in England and for what team
- where he was born and went to school
- how he learnt about British football

- what his ambition was
- how he came to England to play
- how he feels living in England

2 Complete the writing exam strategies below with the verbs in the box.

> wrote   checked   read   wrote   worked out   organised   thought

STRATEGIES

1   I ____ how much time I had to plan, write and check the biography.
2   I ____ all the different ideas I could think of on a piece of paper.
3   I ____ about the type of writing text it was (biography, informal letter, etc) and how this affected my writing and the layout.
4   I ____ a plan and ____ my ideas into paragraphs.
5   When I finished writing, I ____ it. I ____ grammar, spelling and punctuation.

3 Work with a partner and compare the strategies you used. What would you do differently next time?

S11 Laugh

Smile

Complete the questions with the words in the box. Work with a partner and take it in turns to ask and answer the questions.

> jokes   laugh   comedy   comedian

a) When did you last ____ out loud?
b) Are there any ____ programmes on TV you particularly like?
c) Who is your favourite ____?
d) Do you know any good ____?

Reading

1 Work with a partner. Read the title of the web page and discuss what you think the answer to this question is.

2 Check you understand the words in the box. Read the web page and complete the text with these words.

> bonds (verb)   trust (noun)   relief   seventeen   relationships

@ Laughter

Address: @ http://www.laughter

WHY DO WE LAUGH?

The average adult laughs (a) ____ times a day. But why do we do it and what exactly is the purpose of laughter? Anthropologists believe that laughter developed in humans to help us form (b) ____. Experts think the first human laughter was to show (c) ____ when danger had passed. This laughter relaxed the mind and body, but at the same time it made us more vulnerable to another attack. It therefore also indicated (d) ____ between the individuals of the group.

Consequently, laughter has evolved as a way of forming and making stronger human relationships. Laughter usually occurs when people are comfortable with one another, when they feel open and free. The more the people laugh together, the more the group (e) ____. At some time we have all joined in with laughter even when we didn't find anything funny. This is simply because we don't want to appear different. We laugh to say 'I like you and I want to be your friend.'

Internet

(Adapted from *How Stuff Works* website, 2002)

3 Read the web page again and answer these questions.

a) What's the basic reason why laughter developed in humans?
b) What did the first human laughter show?
c) Why did laughter make people more vulnerable to attack?
d) How do people usually feel when they laugh?
e) Why do we sometimes join in with laughter even when we don't find anything funny?

Language awareness

Infinitive of purpose

1 Look at this example from the web page and complete the sentences with the infinitive of an appropriate verb.

*Anthropologists believe that laughter developed in humans **to help** us form relationships.*

a) Humans originally laughed _____ relief when danger had passed.
b) We laugh _____ 'I like you and I want to be your friend.'

2 Complete this sentence with the words in the box.

> purpose   infinitive   why

We use the _____ to express _____: to say _____ we do something or why something happens.

3 Complete the answers using the infinitive of the verbs in the box.

> ~~invite~~   save   help   see   buy   send

a) Why did Maria phone? – _To invite_ us to a party.
b) Where are you going? – To the shop, _____ a newspaper.
c) Why do you want to use the computer? – _____ an e-mail.
d) I phoned you earlier. Where were you? – I went out _____ a friend.
e) Why are you staying in tonight? – _____ money. I've spent too much recently.
f) Why are you learning English? – _____ me get a better job.

4 Translate the answers in 3 into Spanish.

The world's funniest joke?

Listening

1 ▭ 12 In a recent survey 30,000 jokes were told to two million people around the world. Listen to the most popular joke from the survey. Then work with a partner and write down as much of the joke as you can remember.

2 Listen again and check your version of the joke. Do you like the joke?

Phrasal verbs

1 The underlined phrases all have two meanings. Match them to their translations.

1	Can you blow up the balloon for me? I'm out of breath.	a)	volar
2	How did you fall out of the tree?	b)	apagar
3	Can you pick up those books from the floor please?	c)	inflar
4	I'll put the rubbish out. It's going to be collected later today.	d)	coger
5	Terrorists have threatened to blow up parliament.	e)	aprender
6	Stop arguing. You don't want to fall out.	f)	sacar
7	Whenever I go to another country, I try to pick up a few words of their language.	g)	reñir
8	We need to put out the fire quickly before it gets out of control.	h)	caerse

2 Complete these jokes with the phrases in 1.

a) Did you hear about the stupid terrorist? – He tried to _____ a bus and burnt his mouth on the exhaust pipe.
b) Why do birds in a nest always agree? – Because they don't want to _____.
c) Did you _____ the cat _____ before you came to bed? – No, was it on fire?
d) What training do you need to become a rubbish collector? – None, you just _____ it _____ as you go along.

3 Which of these jokes do you like the best? Do you know any other jokes in English? Tell your classmates.

S12 *Pioneer*

Rebel

Work with a partner. Look at the photos and discuss the questions.

- Choose five of these famous pioneers. What do you know about them? Why are they pioneers?
- Which other famous pioneers can you think of?
- Who do you think are the most important pioneers of:
  a) the last ten years?   b) the last hundred years?   c) all time?

Margaret Thatcher

Pelé

Pedro Almodóvar

Bill Gates

J K Rowling

Pablo Picasso

Rigoberta Menchú

Madonna

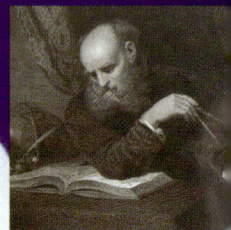
Galileo

Who am I?

Listening 1   🔊 13   You are going to take part in a game called 'Who am I?'. Listen to the seven descriptions and write down the name of each person being described. All the people described are in the photos on this page.

2   Compare your answers with a partner and then check them with your teacher.

Language awareness

Passives 1   🔊 14   Complete the table then listen and check.

Passive	Active
I was criticised by the church …	The church **criticised me** …
The astronomical telescope was invented by Galileo.	a) Galileo ____ **the astronomical telescope**.
b) **Microsoft** ____ by Bill Gates.	Bill Gates **started Microsoft**.

2   Choose the correct alternative.

a) You use the **active/passive** when you want to say what happened to a person or thing.

b) You use the **active/passive** when you want to say what a person or thing did.

For more on passives, see the language reference on page 75.
- **Note:** remember the passive can also be used in other tenses.

3 Complete these sentences about pioneers using the verbs in the box. Put the verb into the most appropriate form: active or passive.

> vote   award   elect   speak   be born   show   move   publish   assassinate   name

  a) He _____ athlete of the century in 1999.
  b) He _____ to Paris when he was twenty-three.
  c) She _____ Prime Minister of the United Kingdom in 1979.
  d) The first Harry Potter book _____ in 1997.
  e) His first film _____ at cinemas in Spain in 1980.
  f) She _____ favourite female singer at the American Music Awards in 1985.
  g) She _____ the Nobel Peace Prize in 1979 for her work helping the poor in Calcutta, India.
  h) He _____ in Stratford-on-Avon, England in 1564.
  i) He _____ the first words from the moon on 20th July 1969.
  j) He _____ by a gunman in Memphis in 1968.

4 Who is each sentence referring to?

5 Translate the following sentences into Spanish. Compare your translations with a partner.

  a) Almodóvar's films are shown all over the world.
  b) Margaret Thatcher was elected Prime Minister three times.
  c) English is spoken here.
  d) This picture was painted by Picasso.
  e) The first part of *Don Quixote* was published in 1605.

Lexis: household items

Work with a partner and answer these questions.

  a) In which room in the house do you usually find these household items? Write each under the appropriate heading. Which of the items do you own?

> microwave   calculator   iron   video recorder   DVD player   scales   hairdryer   headphones   computer
> hi-fi/stereo system   electric toothbrush   hole punch   kettle   stapler   dishwasher

Living room	Study/Office	Bedroom	Bathroom	Kitchen

  b) The items in the box were all once new innovations. Which do you think were the earliest to be invented and which the latest? Match each item with the dates below.

  2500BC   **1800s**   **1900–1950**   **1950–2000**

Guess who

Speaking & writing

1 Choose a famous person and write a 'Who am I?' description about him/her. Use tapescript 13 on pages 189 and 190 as a model.

2 Work in groups and read out your description. Can your classmates guess who is being described?

1 📼 15 Listen to six extracts of different music. Which types of music are they? Choose from the words in the box.

rock	world	disco	electro-pop	reggae	Goth	soul	heavy metal	latin	pop
hip hop	punk	rap	dance/rave/techno	rock 'n' roll	grunge/skate	r 'n' b			

2 Work with a partner and discuss the questions. Use the words in the box or your own.

- Which types of music do you listen to?
- Which types of music do you dance to? When and where?
- What other types of music can you think of?

Reading

1 Read the story behind ABBA's song *Dancing Queen* and answer these questions.

a) When was it written?
b) When was it first performed for the public?
c) When was it officially released?

Abba fact file

The group Abba formed in 1969 in Sweden. They first came to fame with the song *Waterloo* in 1974. They split up at the end of 1982, but the group is as popular as ever. There are numerous tribute bands and their songs are in several films. There is a musical called *Mama Mia*, which includes many of their songs.

Address: http://www.abba

ABBA

Dancing Queen

In August 1975, ABBA had just finished a summer tour of Sweden. But there was no time to relax. At this time groups generally released a new album every year. Björn Ulvaeus (songwriter, guitar, vocals) and Benny Andersson (songwriter, keyboard, vocals) entered the recording studio, where they spent two days recording a few new songs. One of these was called *Boogaloo* because it had strong dance rhythms. This was the song that eventually became *Dancing Queen*. The band knew they had something special and it took several months to complete. This was longer than any other ABBA song. Stig Anderson, Abba's manager, thought of the title *Dancing Queen* and also wrote the lyrics with Björn.

In Sweden, the song was introduced to the public two months before its official release – and it was on a very special occasion. It was at the wedding of King Gustaf of Sweden on 19th June 1976 that *Dancing Queen* was first performed. On 16th August 1976, *Dancing Queen* was finally released. The record sleeve showed ABBA wearing white hats. This photo has become one of the most popular images of the group and is in fact ABBA's favourite picture of themselves. It didn't take long before *Dancing Queen* occupied the number one spot in charts all over the world. It became an instant classic. In April 1977, the song became ABBA's first and only number one in the United States. *Dancing Queen* is ABBA's most famous recording and is generally considered as one of the all-time greatest pop songs. As Agnetha, one of the singers, remembered: 'It's usually difficult to know if a song is going to be successful or not, but *Dancing Queen* was an exception; we knew at once it was going to be massive.'

Internet

(Adapted from *Abba – The Site* website, 2002)

2 Read the text again. Are these sentences true or false?

    a) The original title of *Dancing Queen* was *Boogaloo*.
    b) *Dancing Queen* was written very quickly.
    c) The group didn't like the photograph on the record sleeve.
    d) *Dancing Queen* was ABBA's only number one in the United States.
    e) The group always knew that the song was going to be successful.

3 Read the fact file and the story behind *Dancing Queen* again and write a list of the words and phrases related to music.

    For example: *group, song …*

Dancing Queen

Song

1 Read the lyrics to the song and choose the correct ending to each line in the verses from the words at the bottom of each column.

2 🔲 16 Listen and check.

You can dance, you can jive	You are the Dancing Queen,	You are the Dancing Queen,
Having the time of your life	Young and sweet, only seventeen	Young and sweet, only seventeen
See that girl, watch that scene,	Dancing Queen,	Dancing Queen,
Diggin' the Dancing Queen	Feel the beat from the tambourine	Feel the beat from the tambourine
	You can dance, you can jive,	You can dance, you can jive,
Friday night and the lights are _low_	Having the time of your life	Having the time of your life
Looking out for a place to ____	See that girl, watch that scene,	See that girl, watch that scene
Where they play the right ____,	Diggin' the Dancing Queen	
Getting in the ____		
You come to look for a ____	You're a teaser, you turn them ____	Diggin' the Dancing Queen
Anybody could be that ____	Leave them burning and then you're ____	Diggin' the Dancing Queen
Night is young and the music's ____	Looking out for ____,	Diggin' the Dancing Queen
With a bit of rock ____,	Anyone will ____	Diggin' the Dancing Queen
Everything is ____	You're in the mood for a ____	
You're in the mood for a ____	And when you get the chance …	
And when you get the chance …		

king   music   go   ~~low~~   swing
dance   guy   high   music   fine

gone   on   dance   do
another

3 Read the lyrics again and imagine the scene. Work with a partner and discuss the following questions.

- What kind of person is the girl in the song?
- What does the girl look like?
- What's she wearing?
- Who's she with?
- How's she feeling?

> **jive:** dance, originally a kind of dance popular in the 1950s
> **diggin':** enjoying (informal)
> **swing:** rhythm of the music
> **teaser:** a person who makes someone think they like them
> **turn on:** to make someone feel excited

Speaking Think about a song that you like, perhaps your favourite song. Tell your partner as much as you can about it. Include why you like it, what it is about, what time, place or person it reminds you of and when you last listened to it.

FALSE FRIENDS

Lyrics or *letter*?
Choose the correct alternative.
I love the **lyrics/letter** of this song.

s14 Mobile

Work with a partner. Discuss the following questions.

- Have you got a mobile phone?
- How often do you use it? What do you usually use it for?
- How do you feel about mobile phones? Why?

Reading

1 Work with a partner. Read the title of the article and look at the photo. Discuss what you think the article is about. Then read and check.

Careless talk

TWO WEEKS AGO a friend of mine was almost killed by a man he had never met. My friend was driving carefully across a busy junction when a man in a white van went through a red traffic light at some speed. The man hadn't seen the stop sign because he was talking on his mobile phone. Luckily, my friend wasn't on the phone, had both his hands free and took evasive action. Many other people haven't been so lucky and have been killed by drivers who were chatting, dialling and in a few cases, texting on mobiles.

A study by the Transport Research Laboratory found that a driver reacts 30% more slowly when talking on a mobile phone than when driving a little over the alcohol limit and nearly 50% more slowly than when driving normally.

In the tests at 112 kilometres per hour, the braking distance was 31 metres when fully concentrated, 35 metres with alcohol, 39 metres with a hands-free phone and 45 metres with a hand-held mobile. This shows that people using a hands-free kit react nearly as slowly as those using a hand-held mobile.

So, why isn't the government doing anything to stop people using a mobile while they are driving? At the moment, it's not illegal to use a phone when driving in the UK. The Highway Code, rule 127, suggests you shouldn't use one, but it's not actually against the law. In some countries, however, it is an offence to use a mobile even while the car is stationary. In the UK, there is a lot of opposition to the introduction of a law. Opponents say that if we ban the use of mobiles while driving, we should also ban eating, changing a CD and checking your make-up in the mirror. Research has shown that changing a CD is actually ten times more distracting than using a mobile.

The main problem is that nobody picks up a mobile and thinks 'this will really affect my ability as a driver.' We all think it makes no difference to the way we drive and using a mobile while driving continues to be socially acceptable – in just the same way that drink-driving once was.

(Adapted from *She*, June 2002)

junction: a place where one road crosses another

take evasive action: to do something to avoid a dangerous situation

text (texting): to write and send a message using a mobile phone

ban: to prohibit

2 Read the article again. Are these sentences true or false?

a) Drivers talking on a mobile react more slowly than those driving while a little over the alcohol limit.
b) Using a hands-free kit is a lot safer than using a hand-held mobile phone.
c) In the UK, it's illegal to use a mobile phone while driving.
d) In some countries, it's illegal to use a mobile phone even while the car is stationary.
e) While driving, using a mobile is more distracting than changing a CD.

3 Work with a partner. Discuss the questions.

- How do you feel about the use of mobiles while driving? Has this article changed your opinion?
- What does the law in your country say about using a mobile while driving?
- On what other occasions shouldn't we use a mobile?

Language awareness

Adverbs of manner

1 Look at these examples from the text and complete the sentences with the adverbs in the box.

*My friend was driving **carefully** across a busy junction …*
*… a driver reacts 30% more **slowly** when talking on a mobile phone …*

quickly   easily   heavily   comfortably

a) She passed her exam ____.   c) It's raining ____.
b) Are you sitting ____?   d) He read the books ____.

2 We use adverbs of manner to describe how someone or something does an action. Complete these sentences.

Form: we form adverbs of manner by adding ____ to the adjective. Note what happens to adjectives that end with -*y* and -*ble*. Some adverbs are irregular: *good => well; fast => fast; hard => hard.*
Position in the sentence: adverbs of manner generally go ____ the verb and its object.

3 Change the adjective in brackets into an adverb and put it in the correct place in the sentence.

a) I speak two languages. (fluent)
b) I can sing. (good)
c) I always do my English homework. (careful)
d) I work every day. (hard)
e) I've spoken to my boyfriend/girlfriend today. (brief)
f) I can write text messages. (quick)
g) I speak more in English than in Spanish. (slow)
h) I've been learning English for over one year now. (continuous)
i) I pick up languages. (easy)

4 Work with a partner. Decide if the sentences are true or false for your partner and then ask him or her questions to find out. How well do you know each other?

For example: A: *Do you speak two languages fluently?*
             B: *Yes, I do. Spanish and Italian.*
             A: *Great, I was right. / Really? I thought you only spoke Spanish fluently.*

Reading Read the magazine article and then discuss these questions.

- Do you think the facts and figures are the same in your country?
- Which of the facts and figures do you find the most surprising?
- Do you send and receive text messages? Why / Why not?

GENERATION TXT

TEXT MESSAGING is *the* way to communicate these days. It's instantaneous, cheap, discreet and fun. Everyone is doing it, but the biggest text maniacs are teenagers, very closely followed by twenty-somethings. They send text messages to organise their social lives, make dates, share jokes, pass on gossip and … to flirt. A recent survey showed that 60% of teenagers with mobile phones use text messages to chat people up.

FACTS AND FIGURES
- 75% of all European mobile users regularly send text messages.
- 60% of all text messages sent are sent by women.
- In the UK, a million text messages are sent each hour.
- The highest rate of text messaging is in the Philippines – about 75 million messages are sent each day.

(Adapted from the BBC website, 2002)

S15 *Review 2*

Language reviewed: infinitive of purpose (Unit S11); passives (Unit S12); adverbs of manner (Unit S14)

Lexis: household and office items

1 Can you name the items in the picture? Use the words in the box.

> file   hole punch   Liquid Paper   paperclips   pencil sharpener   Post-it notes   glue
> Sellotape   rubber   ruler   calculator   stapler

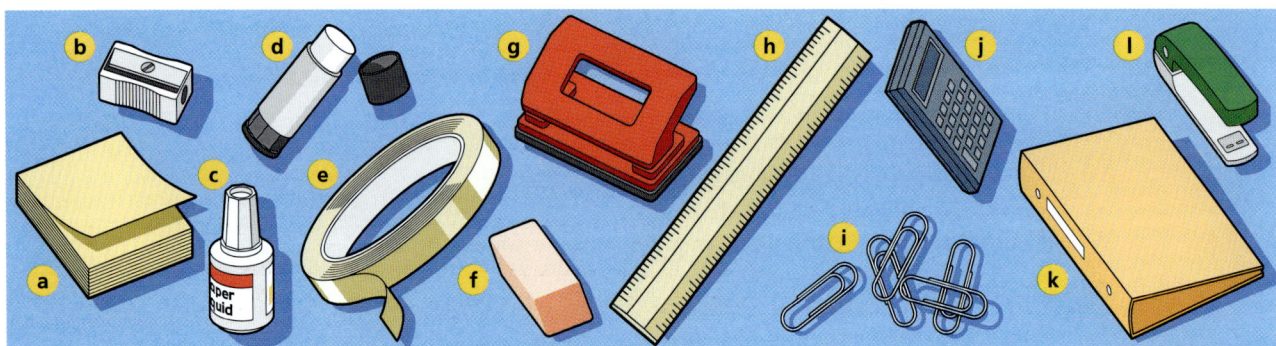

2 Which of these items do you use the most and least often?

From idea to desktop

Listening 1 🔊 17 Listen to how two of the items in the picture were invented. Which two do you hear about?

2 Listen again and choose the correct answer.

a) Spencer Silver created the super weak adhesive in **1960 / 1970 / 1980**.
b) The adhesive was first used **four months / four years / fourteen years** later.
c) When one of the other scientists at 3M started to sing in a church choir, he used pieces of paper to **write down the names of the hymns / write messages to the other people in the choir / find his place in the book**.
d) In 1951 Bette Nesmith Graham **lost her job / got married / got divorced**.
e) She found a job as a **shop assistant / scientist / typist**.
f) Bette sold her product from **work / a friend's shop / her house** for the next 17 years.

Passives 1 Complete the sentences about the items in the recording. Put the verb into the passive.

a) It ____ (invent) by a woman.
b) It ____ (created) accidentally.
c) The product ____ (develop) in the inventor's kitchen and garage.
d) It ____ first ____ (use) to stop bookmarks falling out of a book.
e) The formula and the rights to the product ____ (sell) for $48 million in 1979.
f) It ____ (put) on the market in 1980.

2 Which of the items is each of the sentences in 1 referring to?

Infinitive of purpose

1 Complete the sentences about the items in the picture on page 176. Use the infinitive of the verbs in the box.

> draw   stick   hide   make   write

a) Liquid Paper was invented ____ mistakes.
b) We use Post-it notes ____ messages on.
c) You use a ruler ____ straight lines.
d) You use a hole punch ____ holes in pieces of paper.
e) We use Sellotape ____ things together.

2 Work with a partner. Think of some more everyday items and tell your partner why we use them. Do **not** say the name of the item. Can your partner guess what it is?

For example: A: *You use them to cut pieces of paper.*
B: *Scissors?*
A: *Yes, correct.*

Adverbs of manner

1 Change the adjective in brackets into an adverb and put it into the correct place in the the sentence.

a) Post-it notes were invented. (accidental)
b) The adhesive could be removed. (easy)
c) She typed. (quick)
d) The teacher spoke to her students in English. (very slow)
e) I always put my things away. (tidy)
f) He arranged his papers. (careful)

2 Work with a partner. Write two true sentences about yourself and one false sentence. Each sentence must contain an adverb. Read your sentences to your partner. Can he or she guess which is the false sentence?

For example: *I type very slowly, with only two fingers.*
I ate my lunch quickly today.
I read the newspaper briefly this morning.

Writing

Write a letter or e-mail to a friend and tell them about one of the following:

- an item you have bought recently. For example: a mobile, a computer, a hi-fi, etc
- a comedy film or TV programme you have seen recently
- a pop concert you have been to recently

Remember to use some of the useful words and phrases for letter writing in Unit S8. Write about 100–120 words.

Speaking

Interview your classmates. Choose two of the following topics and prepare 5 or 6 questions to ask different classmates.

- Their favourite comedy film or TV programme. Ask about the storyline, the characters and why it is funny. (Unit S11)
- Their favourite comedy actor. Ask why he/she is funny, which films or TV programmes he/she has been in and about any personal information. (Unit S11)
- A person they really admire. Ask about why they admire him/her so much and about his/her life. (Unit S12)
- An invention they couldn't live without. Ask why it is so important, how often they use it and how they would manage without it. (Unit S12)
- Music they listen to. Ask why they like it, when they started to like it, who their favourite singers and musicians are and when they listen to this music. (Unit S13)
- Their mobile phone. Ask about when and why they use it, when they turn it off, how life would be without it and how they feel about other people using mobile phones. (Unit S14)

Lifestyle

Work with a partner and discuss the questions.

- How important is our diet?
- How has the human diet changed over the years?
- How has your diet changed over the years?
- Look at the box of words often used with *diet*. Which of these can be used to describe your diet?
- What do you eat too much or too little of?
- How could your diet be improved?

diet¹ /ˈdaɪət/ noun ★★
1 [c/u] the food that a person or animal usually eats: Try to eat **a balanced diet**. ◆ *The bird has a diet of nuts and berries*

Words often used with **diet**
*Adjectives often used with **diet** (noun, sense 1)*
■ **balanced, healthy, varied** + DIET: used about foods that are healthy

(From the Macmillan Essential Dictionary)

A nation of fatties

Listening **1** You are going to listen to part of a radio programme called *A nation of fatties*. Before you listen, work with a partner and discuss the questions.

    a) Which country do you think *A nation of fatties* is referring to?
    b) Why are people generally getting fatter?

2 🔊 **18** Listen and check your answers.

3 Listen again and complete this report of the study.

Body Mass Index

BMI = weight (kg)/height (m²)

A survey of British adults and teenagers showed that over (a) _____% of adult men and over (b) _____% of adult women are overweight and unfit. One in (c) _____ adults in Britain is technically obese. Obesity in the UK has tripled in the last (d) _____ years.

Being overweight means there is much more chance of developing (e) _____, diabetes and high blood pressure. Weight-related illnesses cost the National Health Service around £ (f) _____ billion a year.

We are becoming fatter because we eat too much fatty food, drink too much (g) _____ and we don't get enough (h) _____. The average British teenager only gets about (i) _____ hours of physical exercise a week. (j) _____% of teenagers said they didn't do any physical exercise at all.

Language awareness

Reported speech using *said* and *told*

1 Look at the examples in the table and complete the last three sentences.

Actual words	Reported speech
'It's a big problem for both the individual and the country.'	She said that it **was** a big problem for both the individual and the country.
'I **don't do** any physical exercise at all.'	10% of teenagers said they **didn't do** any physical exercise at all.
'I **play** football every week.'	He told me he **played** football every week.
'I**'ll** cook dinner.'	He said he **would** cook dinner.
'I**'m** a student.'	a) She told us she _____ a student.
'We **go** to the gym twice a week.'	b) Peter said that they _____ to the gym twice a week.
'I**'m going** for a run.'	c) He said he _____ for a run.

In its simplest form, we report speech using *said* and *told* and we backshift the verb in the sentence.

- We usually *tell* **somebody something** and we *say* **something**.
  *He **told me** he was a student.*   *He **said** he was a student.*
- We can use *that* before the second clause.
  *She said **that** she would be late.*   or   *She said she would be late.*

2 Look at the picture of Harry below. Read what he said and write each sentence as reported speech. Begin with *He said …* or *He told me …*

a) 'I need to lose some weight.'
b) 'I eat too much fast food.'
c) 'I feel tired all the time.'

d) 'I want to get fitter and healthier.'
e) 'I'm joining a gym.'
f) 'I'll drink less beer.'

Class survey

Writing

1 Write six questions to find out about your classmates' eating habits.

For example: *1 Do you have a healthy diet?*
              2 How often do you eat fresh fruit?

2 Go around the class taking it in turns to ask and answer questions. Make a note of the answers your classmates give you.

3 Write the results of your class survey in a report. Write about 100–150 words. Use the report on page 178 as a model.

Character

Work with a partner and discuss the questions.

- Can the time we were born affect our character and events in our lives?
- Do you believe in western astrology? Why / Why not?
- How often do you read your horoscope in a newspaper or magazine?
- What do you know about Chinese astrology?

Chinese astrology

Reading

1 Look at the pictures of the animals in Chinese astrology. What characteristics do you think each animal has?

2 Find the animal that rules the year you were born and read the character description. How accurate a description of you is it? Discuss this with a partner.

3 Choose three friends or members of your family whose years of birth you know. Read their character descriptions. How accurate are they?

RAT (1924, 1936, 1948, 1960, 1972, 1984, 1996, 2008)

You are determined and ambitious. You make decisions quickly and you always make your ideas work. You are a good organiser. However, your determination and ambition sometimes make you seem selfish.

OX (1925, 1937, 1949, 1961, 1973, 1985, 1997, 2009)

You are patient and dependable. Once you have made a commitment, you always keep your word. You are sometimes too serious about life.

TIGER (1926, 1938, 1950, 1962, 1974, 1986, 1998, 2010)

You are excited by new challenges, unusual places and unexpected events. You trust your instincts and usually follow them. You are confident and a natural leader, but you hate to lose or fail.

RABBIT (1927, 1939, 1951, 1963, 1975, 1987, 1999, 2011)

You have a quiet, calm, peaceful nature. You don't like competition and you hate to be the centre of attention. You are sensitive and always worried about other people's feelings. When you feel depressed, you always keep your thoughts to yourself.

DRAGON (1928, 1940, 1952, 1964, 1976, 1988, 2000)

You have great confidence. You are a very lucky person and you are generally very successful at everything you do. You always try to do your best and you demand high standards from others. You often say exactly what you think and you can appear arrogant. You like the quality things in life.

SNAKE (1929, 1941, 1953, 1965, 1977, 1989, 2001)

You are very lively and energetic. You are extremely intolerant of what you don't like and this means you sometimes can get very angry very quickly. You hate to be told you are wrong.

HORSE (1930, 1942, 1954, 1966, 1978, 1990, 2002)

You are very sociable and you need the company of large and lively groups. You are a very good talker, but you find it hard to keep secrets. You seem independent and confident, but inside you are sometimes quite insecure.

SHEEP (1931, 1943, 1955, 1967, 1979, 1991, 2003)

You are gentle and considerate and you always think before you act. Sometimes you are too sensitive. You enjoy the simple things in life, such as a wonderful view or an inspiring piece of music. You can't stand rules or timetables.

MONKEY (1932, 1944, 1956, 1968, 1980, 1992, 2004)

You are the original party-animal and you are always looking for fun. You adapt well to different situations. You are a good listener and many people confide in you. Secrets are safe in your hands and you are very honest.

ROOSTER (1933, 1945, 1957, 1969, 1981, 1993, 2005)

You love to be the centre of attention and at times you are an exhibitionist. You are funny and you love lively conversation. You are usually well-dressed and you are often critical of other people's appearance. You are very direct and this sometimes gets you into trouble.

DOG (1934, 1946, 1958, 1970, 1982, 1994, 2006)

You are loyal and you are always ready to fight for what you believe in. You have a strong sense of responsibility. However, you frequently worry about this too much; you need to realise that you can't do everything.

PIG (1935, 1947, 1959, 1971, 1983, 1995, 2007)

You are very polite and you have excellent manners in all situations. You are tolerant and peaceful and you hate competition and conflict of any kind. You are a very popular person.

1 The adjectives in the box are all from the *Chinese astrology* text. Work with a partner and decide which of them has: a) a positive meaning; b) a negative meaning; c) both positive and negative meanings.

> loyal considerate direct calm selfish confident honest tolerant ambitious
> arrogant peaceful polite quiet sociable energetic

2 Which is the stressed syllable in each of the adjectives in the box?

For example: *loyal* *considerate* *direct*

3 🔊 19 Listen and check your answers.

Language awareness

Make vs *do*

1 Look at these expressions from the *Chinese astrology* text. Complete the sentences with either *make* or *do*.

a) Once you have _made_ **a commitment,** you …
b) You ____ **decisions** quickly …
c) You always try to ____ **your best** …

2 Add *make* or *do* to complete the following expressions.

a) ____ someone a favour   f) ____ the washing up
b) ____ a new friend   g) ____ the bed
c) ____ well at something   h) ____ some shopping
d) ____ a phone call   i) ____ your homework
e) ____ a coffee   j) ____ dinner for someone

3 Work with a partner. Find out the last time you each did the things in 2. Ask questions to find out more information.

For example: *When did you last do someone a favour?*   *What was it?*
When did you last make a new friend?   *How did you meet?*

Ideal partners

Listening

1 🔊 20 Listen to these people describing their ideal partner. Make notes and then decide which of the animal signs in Chinese astrology they are describing.

2 Put the people in pairs according to Chinese astrology.

Writing

1 Write a description of a celebrity. Include information about the celebrity and their ideal partner. Use tapescript 20 on page 191 to help you.

2 Read your description to your classmates. Do any of the celebrities make good couples?

FALSE FRIENDS

***Still* or *quiet*?**

Which of the underlined words in the sentence means: a) *quieto*; b) *callado*?
The teacher told him to sit (1) still and be (2) quiet.

Spooky

Work with a partner. Discuss the following questions.

- Can you remember any spooky stories, books, films or TV programmes from your childhood?
- Have you ever had a spooky experience?

> **spooky** /spuːki/ adj *informal* strange and frightening
>
> (From the *Macmillan Essential Dictionary*)

Goodbye Mum

Part 1

Reading & listening

1 🔈 **21** Read and listen to this story called *Goodbye Mum*.

A YOUNG MAN was shopping in a supermarket when he noticed that an older woman was following him. She was staring at him sadly. He moved to the next aisle, trying to avoid her, but she followed. She was still staring at him. When he had finished shopping, he found himself behind her in a long check-out queue. Her shopping trolley was completely full. She continued staring and this made him feel very uncomfortable. Finally she spoke. 'I'm sorry for staring,' she said, 'but you look exactly like my son, who died just two weeks ago. He used to do his shopping here. I thought for a moment you were his ghost.' Tears appeared in her eyes. She repeated several times that the young man looked exactly like her son. Then, as she got to the checkout, the woman asked, 'As a favour to me at this terrible time, would you say "Goodbye Mum" to me as I leave? I know it may seem strange, but it would make me feel so much better.' The young man thought for a moment and agreed to her request. She gave him a tearful smile, waved and picked up her heavy bags. 'Goodbye Mum!' he said, waving back.

2 Read and listen again. Put these events from the story in the correct order.

a) She spoke to him.
b) The man noticed a woman staring at him.
c) He said 'Goodbye Mum.'
d) She waved at him.
e) Tears appeared in the woman's eyes.
f) He moved to a different aisle.
g) She asked him to do her a favour.
h) He found himself behind her in the check-out queue.

3 Why did the woman ask him to say 'Goodbye Mum'?

4 Work with a partner and discuss these questions. Write your answers.

a) How did the woman feel as she left the supermarket?
b) How did the man feel about the woman?

You will hear the rest of this story at the end of the unit.

Language awareness

Narrative tenses: past simple, continuous, & perfect

1 Read these extracts from the story *Goodbye Mum*. Complete the table with the letters *a–g*. Write the names of the tenses in the table.

A young man (a) **was shopping** in a supermarket when he (b) **noticed** that an older woman (c) **was following** him.
He (d) **moved** to a different aisle, trying to avoid her, but she (e) **followed**.
When he (f) **had finished** shopping, he (g) **found** himself behind her in a long check-out queue.

Use		Examples	Tense
1	to show a background activity in progress	*a*	
2	to show a short, quickly finished action in the past	*b*	
3	to show that one past event happened before another past event		

2 Complete the story *Fairy tale ending* by putting the verbs in brackets into the correct past tense.

Fairy tale ending

Mary Tufnell was born in Cleveland, Ohio in 1920. As a child, her favourite possession was a book of fairy tales, which she (a) ____ (read) all the time. When she was ten, she (b) ____ (move) to Paris with her family. As they only took one small trunk between them, Mary wasn't allowed to include her book.

Many years later, when she was in her seventies, Mary (c) ____ (think) about what to buy as a birthday present for her ten-year-old granddaughter. For some reason she remembered a second-hand bookshop she (d) ____ (visit) a few weeks before. She (e) ____ (decide) to go there to see what she could find. She (f) ____ (look) in the children's section of the bookshop when suddenly she (g) ____ (begin) to laugh. At the end of the shelf there was a copy of the book of fairy tales that she (h) ____ (love) so much as a child back in the United States. When she opened the book, she (i) ____ (find) her name and old address inside. It was the very copy she (j) ____ (have) as a child.

3 ▭ **22** Listen and check your answers.

Goodbye Mum

Part 2

▭ **23** You are going to hear the end of the story *Goodbye Mum*. Before you listen, work with a partner and discuss what happened in the first part of the story. What were your answers to the questions in 3 and 4 on page 182? After you have listened to the end of the story, answer these questions again.

Writing a narrative

1 Write a spooky story. Choose from the titles in the box or one of your own. Organise your story into paragraphs and try to include a surprising ending. Use the *Goodbye Mum* story as a model. Remember to include the narrative tenses you have practised in this unit. Write about 100–120 words.

LANGUAGE TOOLBOX

When …
Then …
After …
As soon as …
Suddenly, …

> Honeymoon couple   Good night, my sweet   Henry   The hitchhiker   The dream
> The cellar   The new neighbours   The babysitter   The anniversary   Doll's house
> The visitor   The dark wood   The voice   Red room   The window   Land of toys

2 Take it in turns to read out your stories. Which story has the most surprising ending?

S19 *Eye*

Wheels

Work with a partner. Look at the photo and discuss the following questions.

a) What is it? What is it called? Where is it? How old is it? Why was it built?
b) Have you ever been on it or do you know anyone who has been on it?
c) Would you like to go on it?

Reading   **1**   Read the text about the British Airways London Eye and check your answers to a) above.

(Adapted from the British Airways London Eye website, 2002)

@ London Eye

Address: @ http://www.londoneye

World of THE EYE

THE BRITISH AIRWAYS LONDON EYE (often called just The Eye) represents the turning of time and celebrates London's past and looks forward to its future. It is a beautiful new landmark and it gives its passengers a completely new perspective of one of the world's major cities.

The Eye was constructed piece by piece throughout Europe. It took seven years from initial idea to final construction. As it was the biggest observation wheel ever designed, it couldn't be built in one place. The main structure, 135 metres in diameter, was built in Holland. The thirty-two capsules, each capable of carrying up to twenty-five passengers, were made in France. The other parts of the wheel were made in the Czech Republic, Germany and Italy. Consequently, it is truly a European project. After all the components had been made, The Eye was assembled at its site next to the River Thames. Each piece was sailed up the river by boat and The Eye was then constructed horizontally on platforms over the river. Finally, the 1,900-tonne structure was lifted into its final position in time for the year 2000 millennium celebrations.

The specially designed capsules travel at 0.26 metres per second and are designed to help you see out from all sides. Because they are attached on the outside of the wheel, the structure doesn't obscure the view. The design is unique. Your 'flight' lasts 30 minutes and on a clear day, you will be able to see for 25 miles (40 kilometres) – as far as Heathrow Airport and Windsor Castle.

Internet

---

2   <u>Underline</u> three facts that you learn about the London Eye and compare them with a partner.

3   Read the text again and complete the fact file.

London Eye fact file		
Location	a)	____
Countries where constructed	b)	____, ____, ____, ____, ____
Diameter	c)	____ metres
Weight	d)	____ tonnes
Speed	e)	____ metres per second
Flight time (time to revolve 360°)	f)	____ minutes
Number of capsules	g)	____
Capsule capacity	h)	____ passengers
Viewing distance	i)	____ miles (____ km)

Listening

1 ⏺ **24** You are going to listen to three people talking about the London Eye. Listen to their conversation and choose the correct name in each sentence.

a) **Peter / Emily / Tony** hasn't been on the London Eye.
b) **Peter / Emily / Tony** had a great time on the London Eye.
c) **Peter / Emily / Tony** was disappointed by the London Eye.
d) **Peter / Emily / Tony** thinks there should be more information about the buildings and sights you see.
e) **Peter / Emily / Tony** took some photos from the London Eye.
f) **Peter / Emily / Tony** is thinking of going on the London Eye for a second time.

2 Listen again and complete the sentences using the words and phrases in the box.

I don't agree   Don't you think   think
I agree   yeah, but   In my opinion   think

a) What did you ____ of it? (Peter)
b) ____, Tony? (Emily)
c) Well, ____ … to be honest I was very disappointed. ____ it's a bit boring actually. (Tony)
d) I also ____ they should tell you what to look out for. (Tony)
e) ____. I thought it was wonderful. (Emily)
f) It must be disappointing on a cloudy day – ____ with you there. (Emily)

3 Do you think Peter will go on the London Eye? Why / Why not?

Language awareness

Opinions

1 Complete the table with expressions in the box. Listen to or read tapescript 24 on page 191 again to help you.

I think …   I don't think …   Yeah, but …   I agree (with …)   Don't you think …?
What do you think of …?

Asking for an opinion	Giving an opinion	Agreeing	Disagreeing
What's your opinion of …?	In my opinion, … To me, …	Yeah, and … I totally agree (with …)	I disagree (with …) I totally disagree (with …) I see what you mean, but …

2 Work in small groups. Choose some of the statements below. Ask for, give and discuss your opinions of them.

'Top footballers and other sportspeople are paid too much.'
'Private education is better than state education.'
'Children shouldn't watch more than one hour of TV a day.'
'Everyone should learn English.'
'We rely too much on computers.'
'Everyone should try to spend at least a year in another country.'

Developing exam strategies 2

Language reviewed: narrative tenses: past simple, continuous, perfect (Unit S18); opinions (Unit S19)

In this unit you will continue to develop your exam strategies by:

- practising different skills and exercise types found in English exams
- reflecting on how you did these exercises
- thinking about other ways you could approach them
- looking at general strategies for the final exam

Reading comprehension

I was a coffeeholic

It was a long-lasting and very public love affair. But it was bad for me and it had to end. I'm finished with coffee and I'm not going back.

I had been thinking about stopping for ages. But every 5 time I read one story about how bad coffee was for us, I read another about how good it can be. Also, I felt that worrying about coffee was worse for my health than actually drinking it. So I stopped worrying and continued drinking.

10 As time passed, single macchiatos turned into doubles and lattes became double espresso latte grandes. I needed more and more coffee to survive the day.

One sunny morning last summer while I was drinking my third cup of coffee, I realised I was addicted. I 15 decided to stop.

I will always remember the first day of Life Without Coffee. It wasn't just the chemicals I had left behind. It was also the ritual of being a coffee drinker: a cup or two to wake me up in the morning and then another 20 when I arrived at work. It was the perfect excuse for a chat with workmates and coffee was the reward for finishing each piece of work during the day. Sadly, this was all gone.

The next two days were the worst of my life. I couldn't 25 move. I didn't want to move. I just wanted to sit in my armchair. My friends started asking me if I was okay. Then, as if by magic, everything suddenly changed. I felt alive again and full of energy. But I was more calm and focused than I had been. Friends and colleagues have 30 complimented me about the post-coffee me.

So, do I miss coffee? Of course I do. I miss everything from the first-thing-in-the-morning buzz to the late-in-the-evening after-dinner cappuccino. What I don't miss, however, is the dependence I had on coffee and the 35 longing that was only satisfied by having another cup. I was a coffeeholic.

1 Read the text. Are these sentences true or false? Write *T* or *F* in the boxes.

a) The writer only read bad things about coffee. ☐
b) As time passed she drank more coffee. ☐
c) She never drank coffee at work. ☐
d) She felt great for the first two days after she stopped drinking coffee. ☐
e) She became a calmer person after she stopped drinking coffee. ☐
f) She misses drinking coffee. ☐

2 Find words or phrases in the text which mean the same as the following.

a) unable to stop doing something (paragraph 4)
b) something you do regularly and in the same way each time (paragraph 5)
c) friendly conversation (paragraph 5)
d) something good that you receive because of something you have done (paragraph 5)
e) people who work in the same organisation or department as you (paragraph 6)
f) strong feeling of pleasure or excitement (paragraph 7)

3 Read the reading exam strategies below. Which strategies did you use for: a) the true/false exercise? b) the vocabulary exercise? c) both exercises? Match the strategies with the reading exercises and then compare your answers with a partner.

1 I read the text quickly to get a general idea (gist).
2 I read the text quickly to look for specific information (scan).
3 I looked for words in the text that had a connection with the statements.
4 I didn't worry about unfamiliar words. I didn't try to understand every word.
5 I checked the form/function of the words I had to find in the text.
6 I substituted the word for the definition and checked they worked in the sentence.
7 I read the sentence and looked at specific words to give me clues.
8 I read the specific information carefully and <u>underlined</u> it.
9 (add others you used)

4 Work with a partner and compare the strategies you used. What would you do differently next time?

Speaking

1 Work with a partner. Choose one of these topics. Take it in turns to talk about the topic.

- A wonderful dish or some food you ate.
- A person you met for the first time.
- A strange experience you had.
- A day out with a friend.

2 Read the speaking exam strategies below. Tick (✓) the ones you used in the previous exercise. Circle the ones you need to use next time. Then work with a partner and compare the strategies you used.

- Before the exam, practise talking about different topics in pairs or groups.
- Before the exam, prepare and revise the specific language you will need to interact: how to interrupt, change the subject, agreeing and disagreeing, etc.
- Be prepared to talk about yourself (background, job or studies, interests, etc).
- When you are given a task think about:
  1 what you want to talk about
  2 the questions you will ask / may be asked
  3 the language you will need
- Speak clearly and listen carefully.
- Show that you can interact, but do not monopolise the conversation.
- If your partner does not say much, try to help them participate.
- If you don't know a word, try to use a synonym or explain the word in English.
- When you don't understand something, ask the person to repeat it.

Before & during the exam

1 Read the general exam strategies below. Put each strategy under the appropriate headings.

A	B
Before the exam	**During the exam**

1   Find out as much as you can about the different parts of the exam.
2   <u>Underline</u> important instructions and information.
3   Organise your study time.
4   Get information about the type of questions.
5   Read the instructions on the exam paper carefully.
6   Don't spend too much time on each question.
7   Listen carefully to any oral instructions.
8   Find out the time you are recommended to spend on each part/question.
9   Practise exam questions.
10 Check you have answered all the questions you need to.

2 Can you add any other tips to this list?

Tapescripts

^{S}1 Them

📼 01

a) What's your name?
b) What do you do? / What do you do for a living?
g) Where were you born?
h) How old are you?
i) Have you got any brothers or sisters?
j) Have you got any children?
m) Do you speak English outside class?
o) What do you like doing in your spare time?

📼 02

c) What do you <u>study</u>? / What are you <u>studying</u>?
d) Where do you <u>work</u>?
e) Where do you <u>live</u>?
f) Where are you <u>from</u>? / Where do you <u>come</u> from?
k) Why are you learning <u>English</u>?
l) When did you first start to <u>learn</u> it?
n) How often do you <u>speak</u> it?
p) What's your favourite <u>music</u>?

^{S}2 Here

📼 03

A

What's it like? Well, you know, this is without any doubt my favourite city in Spain. It's really terrific. I always tell visitors to Spain you have to see this place.

In summer the mornings are cool and fresh, whereas the afternoons are always extremely hot. From mid-June to the end of September you really can't do anything.

The people are very friendly. The light here is quite spectacular and the colours are amazing. The sky is so blue. Sometimes it looks like a professional photograph from a magazine, and you ask yourself: can it really be that blue? And if you're there in the springtime you can smell the orange blossom all around the city: it's very romantic.

Definitely, Seville is a place which I keep going back to year after year.

B

Ah, yes, this really is one of the most fascinating cities in Europe. Okay, if you want to try a little cultural tourism, visit some of the world-famous museums and galleries or walk through the historic parks and gardens. But the city is also well-known for its exciting nightlife. Restaurants, theatres, bars, nightclubs, shows – you'll never go to bed! Believe me, this is the place if you want to enjoy yourself. Madrid has got everything!

C

I was surprised because before I went there, a lot of people had told me it was a very dark city – very ugly, dirty, and … well, generally they had very negative impressions of the place. Some of the people I talked to were, in fact, from the city. Others were people who had been there on visits – sometimes as tourists, sometimes on business. Yes, like I said, I was very surprised. To be honest, I found it a very elegant city.

Okay, the weather was bad. In fact, I think it rained most of the weekend I was there. But the old town is very charming – it has a lot of atmosphere.

And of course, there's the Guggenheim Museum. It's a beautiful building from the outside, though I have to say the exhibition was rather unimpressive.

I was only in Bilbao for a weekend, which isn't a very long time. I think I'd like to go back. Yes, definitely.

D

This city is unique. It's got a special magic – and so many things to see. If you want to get a taste of Gaudí's strange architecture, then you've got to visit La Pedrera, Parque Güell and the church of La Sagrada Família. But it's also important to experience the modernist buildings, the Gothic quarter, and also the atmosphere that you can feel when you walk around the Ramblas, the Paseo de Gracia or Port Vell, the old port. Ultimately it's the mix of sea and mountains that makes this city so wonderful! The great thing about Barcelona is that it has all the marvellous facilities of a large city but with all the unforgettable charm of a small town.

^{S}3 Secrets

📼 04

(See page 152.)

📼 05

depressed	wanted
lived	interested
opened	locked
decided	disappointed
looked	enjoyed
hated	shocked
started	excited
organised	
needed	
surprised	

^{S}4 Sport

📼 06

1
A: Would you like to start?
B: Yes, okay.

2
A: We've answered all the questions, so I think we've finished.
B: Yeah, I think we have.

3
A: What do we have to do?
B: Answer the questions, I think.

4
A: So who's going to start?
B: You can start.
A: No, *you* start.
B: Okay.

5
A: Shall I start?
B: I don't mind. You go ahead.

6
A: What are we supposed to do?
B: I don't know. Ask Paul.

7
A: I enjoyed doing that activity.
B: Oh, I didn't. I found it a bit boring, actually.
A: Oh, really?

^{S}5 Review 1

📼 07

(See page 157.)

^{S}6 Souvenirs

📼 08

(See page 159.)

^{S}7 Work

📼 09

(A = Alison; B = Ben; C = Cathy; D = Dave)

A: You know, that's quite a difficult question for me. When I was a child, I really liked dressing up – you know, putting on my mum's shoes and hats and my big sister's dresses. And I loved Art at school. So for a long time I wanted to become a fashion designer but when I was at college I organised the music for the discos. I've always enjoyed listening to music so now I'm a full-time DJ and I work in Ibiza every summer, which is fantastic! I'm still interested in fashion but I haven't had much time over the last few years to do any designing.

B: Oh, when I was young I knew exactly what I wanted to be. You see, I've always been good at sport – basketball, cricket, athletics, football … but tennis was my real love when I was a child. Anyway, I wasn't good enough to join the local tennis club so I began to play more football. I was lucky one of the big clubs saw me play and thought I was good enough so they signed me up. I became a professional footballer after I left school. I've had a good career, but in a few years' time, when I retire from the game, I'd like to do something completely different. I'd like to train to be a pilot. I really love flying.

C: Oh, I don't know. When I was small, I thought of becoming a nurse and working in Africa. Travelling to a foreign country, helping people – it all sounded very exciting! However, some years later, I joined a drama group at my secondary school and I became really interested in the theatre. I acted in lots of plays and performed in lots of shows. I had a great time. Anyway, after school I studied drama, and I've been an actress since then. It's a tough job but I love it.

D: That's an easy question for me. You see, I've always loved animals. When I was little I had lots of pets – you know, dogs and cats and birds and rabbits and goldfish and things. Our house was like a zoo! But I really loved looking after them all. So, even when I was a little boy I knew that I wanted to work with animals. I'm thirty-two now and I've been a qualified vet for five years. For me it's the perfect job.

ˢ8 Spend

🔲 10

(Interviewer = I; A = Anna)

I: Okay, Anna: first question. Where did you go on your last holiday and how much did it cost?
A: I went to Portugal, and, with spending money, it was around £1,000. But I spent quite a lot of that on shoes and perfume, duty frees and gifts.
I: What's your worst-ever buy?
A: For my honeymoon in Cyprus, I spent £150 on a black designer bikini that broke on the first day.
I: What's your best bargain?
A: I was at a car boot sale, and there was a Ford Escort van that was on sale for £180, so I bought it. I had a furniture business at the time, and I used it for transporting the furniture.
I: Are you a credit card person or a cash person?
A: Always cash, although I have a Mastercard I never use.

I: What do you feel you waste your money on?
A: My mobile phone. It costs me around £80 a month. My home phone is only about £20.
I: How much do you spend on lunch each week?
A: Nothing. I eat in my restaurant every day of the week.
I: Where does most of your money go?
A: On my five-year-old daughter's clothes and outings.
I: How much do you spend on clothes?
A: I tend to do a big shop every three months and spend about £300.
I: What's the most expensive present you've ever bought someone?
A: A £200 PlayStation for my daughter.
I: So your restaurant must make a profit if you can spend all this money!
A: [laughs]
I: Thank you, Anna, for answering our questions.

ˢ10 Developing exam strategies 1

🔲 11

(I = Interviewer; JK = Joseph Kome)

I: Joseph, did you watch much English football as a child? And did you support an English team?
JK: No, I didn't watch much English football at all. In Senegal we got a sports programme on Sunday evenings which showed English football. But, in fact they didn't show much of the matches, just the goals, really. I didn't support any English team at the time – I didn't know enough about them. But I always dreamt of playing in an English team.
I: How did your move to England happen?
JK: Well, my agent organised it all. I had been playing for my local club for about six years and I felt I needed a change. So when my agent told me that this club was having a football trial for new players I flew to England for the trial. When they offered me a contract for three years, I said yes immediately.
I: What were your first impressions of English football, and how have those impressions changed?
JK: Well, at first I was shocked. The game is so fast and aggressive here. You have to run and run, and you don't get much time to rest during the game. In my first matches I often got very tired before the end. But my coach and my teammates helped me adjust. Mmm … Then, after a month or two I really began to enjoy the English way of playing.
I: You speak English very well. Where did you learn it?

JK: Well, I studied English at school, and I loved watching English films and programmes on TV. And then I had lessons with a tutor in Senegal before I came to England. Now I mostly learn new words from the rest of the players. I still find some accents difficult to understand, though.
I: What do you like and dislike about living in England?
JK: Well, I like the relaxed lifestyle. On the roads, for example, people here are patient. They take their time. In my hometown everybody's in a hurry – shouting or beeping their horns at each other all the time. Things in England are far more expensive, though – food, clothes, buying a house …
I: What do you like least about it?
JK: Well, when I first came to England I always thought that English fans supported you all the time, even when you weren't playing very well. But now I know they really can turn against you after a couple of bad matches. So I guess football supporters are the same everywhere, aren't they?

ˢ11 Laugh

🔲 12

Two hunters are in a wood when one of them falls to the ground. He doesn't seem to be breathing and his eyes are closed. The other hunter takes his mobile phone and calls the emergency services. He tells the operator 'My friend is dead! What can I do?' The operator in a calm voice says 'Stay calm. I can help. First, we must make sure your friend is dead.' There is silence, then a gun shot is heard. The man's voice comes back on the phone. He says 'Okay, now what?'

ˢ12 Pioneer

🔲 13

1

I was born in 1965 in the United Kingdom. I wrote my first story, called *Rabbit*, when I was six and I have been writing ever since. My first book, about a boy who is a wizard, was published in 1997. I have written several more books about this boy wizard since then – the fourth book in the series became the fastest-selling book of all time. People say I have done more to encourage children to read than any other writer. My books have been awarded many literary prizes, they have been translated into about 30 languages and they have been made into very successful films. I am known by my initials, but my real name is Joanne Kathleen. Who am I?

2

I was born in 1881 in Spain. In my late teens, I studied at the Academy of Fine Arts in Barcelona, where my father was a professor. I moved to Paris when I was twenty-three. I helped to pioneer the art movement called 'cubism'. I went on to become one of the most famous and successful painters of the twentieth century. Who am I?

3

I was born in 1564. I was a great mathematician, astronomer, and physicist. I invented the astronomical telescope. I was criticised by the church in Italy for supporting the theory that the Earth revolved around the Sun. Who am I?

4

I was born in 1949 in Calzada de Calatrava in Spain. When I was 16, I left my friends and family and I moved to Madrid because I wanted to study cinema and become a film maker. I soon saved enough money to buy my first camera and I started making films. My first professional film was shown at cinemas in Spain in 1980. I have become one of the world's most famous film writers and directors and my films are shown all over the world. Who am I?

5

I was born in 1955. I became interested in computers when I was twelve and I started my first company when I was at school. I wrote the computer language BASIC while I was at university. I didn't finish my studies because I left to start another software company. I became a billionaire at 31. Who am I?

6

I was born in the UK in 1925. I studied science at Oxford University and worked as a chemist before becoming a politician in 1959. I was elected Prime Minister of my country in 1979 and I won three consecutive elections before I resigned in 1990. I was Europe's first woman Prime Minister. Who am I?

7

I played my first professional football match when I was sixteen. 1,362 matches later I had scored 1,280 goals, a world record. I played in four World Cup tournaments and my country won three of them. I became a national hero and I retired from football in 1977. I was named athlete of the century in 1999. Who am I?

📼 **14**

a) Galileo invented the astronomical telescope.
b) Microsoft was started by Bill Gates.

ˢ13 Pop

📼 **15**

[instrumental extracts]

📼 **16**

Dancing Queen **by Benny Andersson, Stig Anderson, Björn Ulvaeus**

You can dance, you can jive
Having the time of your life
See that girl, watch that scene
Diggin' the Dancing Queen

Friday night and the lights are low
Looking out for a place to go
Where they play the right music
Getting in the swing
You come to look for a king

Anybody could be that guy
Night is young and the music's high
With a bit of rock music
Everything is fine
You're in the mood for a dance

And when you get the chance …

You are the Dancing Queen
Young and sweet, only seventeen
Dancing Queen
Feel the beat from the tambourine
You can dance, you can jive
Having the time of your life
See that girl, watch that scene
Diggin' the Dancing Queen

You're a teaser, you turn them on
Leave them burning and then
you're gone
Looking out for another
Anyone will do
You're in the mood for a dance

And when you get the chance …

You are the Dancing Queen
Young and sweet, only seventeen
Dancing Queen
Feel the beat from the tambourine
You can dance, you can jive
Having the time of your life
See that girl, watch that scene
Diggin' the Dancing Queen

Diggin' the Dancing Queen
Diggin' the Dancing Queen
Diggin' the Dancing Queen

ˢ15 Review 2

📼 **17**

1

Everyone knows what they are, most people use them and lots of people love them. But they were not a planned product. They were created accidentally. They were invented by a man named Spencer Silver. In 1970, he was working in the 3M research laboratories trying to develop a new, strong adhesive. By chance he created an adhesive which stuck to objects, but which could also be removed easily. It was super weak instead of super strong! No one knew what to do with this new adhesive so it

wasn't used but Silver didn't forget about it.

Four years later, one of the other scientists from 3M research laboratories began to sing in the church choir. He used pieces of paper to find his place in the hymn book, but they kept falling out of the book. Silver remembered his invention from four years earlier and suggested that his friend put some of this weak adhesive on his pieces of paper. It worked; the pieces of paper stayed in place, but they could be removed easily without damaging the pages of the hymn book. The product was put on the market in 1980 and today it is one of the most popular office products.

2

This product was invented by a woman called Bette Nesmith Graham. In 1951, she got divorced and she needed to go to work to support herself and her son. She found work as a typist, but unfortunately she wasn't a very good one – she typed very slowly and made lots of mistakes. She used her kitchen and garage as a laboratory and factory, to develop a white paint that she used to hide her mistakes. Soon, other secretaries and office workers began to buy this from her. Bette continued to work as a secretary and at the same time she studied business. She decided to call her product 'Liquid paper' and she continued to sell it from her house for the next 17 years. In 1979, she sold the formula and the rights to Liquid Paper for $48 million. Bette's son became even more famous than she did. He is Michael Nesmith; a member of the sixties' pop group The Monkees.

ˢ16 Diet

📼 **18**

(I = Interviewer; P = Professor Nicola James)

I: … and now let me introduce Professor Nicola James, expert on nutrition and diet. I understand there are some rather worrying findings from a recent study on the nation's weight.

P: That's right. The study revealed that Britain is becoming a nation of fatties. Over 60% of adult men and 50% of adult women are overweight and unfit. And one in five adults in Britain is technically obese. The research also revealed that obesity in the United Kingdom has tripled in the last 10 years. We are putting on the pounds faster than any other European country. And if we continue at this rate, by 2010 we will equal the United States, where over a quarter of all adults are obese.

I: You mentioned being 'overweight' and being 'technically obese'. What's the difference?

P: Well, it depends on your Body Mass Index or your BMI. A BMI over 25 is overweight, and a BMI over 30 is obese.

I: And what are the main problems of being overweight?

P: It's a big problem for both the individual and the country. Basically, being overweight increases the risk of illness and early death. There is much more chance of developing heart disease, diabetes and high blood pressure. It's also an economic problem for the country. Weight-related illnesses cost the National Health Service around £1.5 billion a year.

I: So, why are we becoming fatter?

P: Basically because of our lazy lifestyle and our poor diet. We eat too much fatty food, drink too much alcohol and we don't get enough exercise. We spend too much time watching television, using the Internet and travelling by car. The average British teenager only gets about 10 hours of physical exercise a week – that's all physical activity including walking between classes! 10% of teenagers said they did no physical exercise at all. To be as active as our grandparents, we would have to run a marathon every week …

S17 Character

📼 19

(See page 181.)

📼 20

(P = pig; M = monkey; R = rabbit; D = dragon)

1

P: My ideal partner is someone who is quiet and calm, … peaceful even, … someone who definitely doesn't like to be the centre of attention. I can't stand people who are always telling everyone else about themselves and about their problems. I like people who are sensitive and caring. And I really don't like competitive people at all.

2

M: My ideal boyfriend is self-confident and successful, not just in his job, but in all other aspects of his life. Yes, … that's the most important thing for me. Well, hopefully he's quite rich as well. He should demand high standards of himself and of the people and things around him. I like people who appreciate quality, … you know, good restaurants, clothes, nightclubs and the like, … and expensive gifts for me of course. He's probably a bit older than me.

3

R: Any boyfriend of mine must enjoy the peace and quiet like I do. He must be tolerant of others, … someone who doesn't feel the need to be critical or competitive all the time. But, the most important thing for me, and this may seem a little old-fashioned, is that he's always polite and has good manners. That really is the most important thing for me.

4

D: I love party people, … people that are always looking for fun. I'm a very successful business man and I meet lots of people through work, so my partner must be someone who can adapt and know how to act in different situations. She must be someone I can trust and be good at keeping secrets as I'm the world's worst gossip.

S18 Spooky

📼 21

(See page 182.)

📼 22

Mary Tufnell was born in Cleveland, Ohio in 1920. As a child, her favourite possession was a book of fairy tales, which she read all the time. When she was ten, she moved to Paris with her family. As they only took one small trunk between them, Mary wasn't allowed to include her book.

Many years later, when she was in her seventies, Mary was thinking about what to buy as a birthday present for her ten-year-old granddaughter. For some reason she remembered a second-hand bookshop she had visited a few weeks before. She decided to go there to see what she could find. She was looking in the children's section of the bookshop when suddenly she began to laugh. At the end of the shelf there was a copy of the book of fairy tales that she had loved so much as a child back in the United States. When she opened the book, she found her name and old address inside. It was the very copy she had had as a child.

📼 23

Goodbye Mum Part 2
The young man was thinking about what had happened when the cashier told him his bill was £150. 'There must be a mistake,' the young man said, pointing at his three items. 'Yes,' the cashier said, 'but your mother said you would pay for hers too.'

S19 Eye

📼 24

(P = Peter; E = Emily; T = Tony)

P: We're thinking of going on the London Eye when we are in London tomorrow. You two have both been on it, haven't you? What did you think of it?

E: Oh Peter, it was fantastic. You'll have a great time. Don't you think, Tony?

T: Well, yeah, but … to be honest I was very disappointed. In my opinion it's a bit boring actually. All you do is stand in a big capsule and move round for thirty minutes. I was expecting much more.

P: What do you mean?

T: Well, for a start it goes very slowly and I also think they should tell you what to look out for – there should be more information about the buildings and sights you can see. That would make it much more interesting.

E: I don't agree. I thought it was wonderful. You see London in a completely different way. It's a totally unique and personal experience. I didn't want anyone to give me more information – that would make it too commercial. To me, what made it fun was that you could move around and look at whatever you wanted. I took some brilliant photos.

T: Well, it was raining and cold when I went so we couldn't see very far and I couldn't take any photographs. Jane and I also spent the whole day arguing.

P: Oh dear, well no wonder you didn't enjoy it.

E: It must be disappointing on a cloudy day – I agree with you there. You have to go on a sunny, clear day. You should try it again Tony but next …

P: Okay, you two. So, should I go or not?

E: Yes, don't miss it!

T: Well, I suppose it is something different. Yeah, why not? Perhaps I'll come with you. What's the weather forecast for tomorrow?

P: Actually, I don't think it's going to be very nice …

Macmillan Education
Between Towns Road, Oxford OX4 3PP
A division of Macmillan Publishers Limited
Companies and representatives throughout the world

International 978-0-333-92385-6
Level II   978-0-333-99903-5

Project management by Desmond O'Sullivan, ELT Publishing Services.
Designed by Jackie Hill, 320 Design.
Illustrated by Martin Chatterton pp127, 128; Rebecca Halls pp62, 63,
77, 122, 123; Ed McLachlan pp17, 32, 42, 57, 88, 92, 116; Julian
Mosedale pp24, 39, 54, 91, 121; David Shephard pp23, 59; Mark
Thomas p117; Kim Williams pp124, 126.
Cover design by Andrew Oliver.
Cover painting *After Visiting David Hockney* © Howard Hodgkin.

Authors' acknowledgements
We would like to thank all our colleagues at the Lake School, Oxford,
for their help and continued support; in particular, Pete Maggs,
whose thoughtful comments on work in progress were much
appreciated. Thanks also go to our pre-intermediate students who
have kept us focused at all times on what works in the classroom
(and made sure that we disregarded everything else).
We are especially grateful to Helena Gomm and Jon Hird for the
Inside Out Teacher's Book, to Pete Maggs for the weekly *Inside Out*
e-lessons, to Guy Jackson for running the *Inside Out* website at
www.insideout.net, which has finally come of age, and to everybody
involved in the *Inside Out* Resource Pack: a great team!
At Macmillan Education we would like to thank Sue Bale (publishing
director), David Riley (publisher), and Pippa McNee (picture
researcher). We would also like to thank Alyson Maskell and Celia
Bingham (freelance editors), Jackie Hill (freelance designer), Helen
Reilly (freelance picture researcher), Paulette McKean (freelance
permissions editor), as well as James Richardson and Vince Cross
(freelance audio producers). Thanks also go to the production and
marketing teams who have worked so hard to make *Inside Out* what
it is.
Once again, we reserve the biggest thank you of all for Desmond
O'Sullivan (freelance project manager). We are indeed privileged to
be working with such a talented and committed professional – long
may it continue! Thanks for everything, Des.
In addition, we must thank our families, without whose support and
understanding none of this would have been possible.
We would also like to thank Thalia Carr (The Swan School, Oxford),
Jenny Johnson (International House, Barcelona) Beth Neher
(International House, London) and Katarzyna Kowalczyk (Macmillan
Polska) for their very helpful comments.

The authors and publishers would like to thank the following for
permission to reproduce their material:
Extract from 'e-How to remember names' by Valerie Singer from
www.ehow.com, reprinted by permission of Blue Frogg Enterprises.
Lyric of *Stand By Me*, composed by Jerry Leiber / Mike Stoller / Ben E.
King. Produced by kind permission of Jerry Leiber Music / Mike Stoller
Music / Mike & Jerry Music LLC. Extract from 'They were the happiest
couple in showbiz … but then it all went wrong' by Polly Graham
from *The Mirror* 06.02.01, reprinted by permission of Mirror
Syndication International. Lyric of *Suspicious Minds*. Words and music
by Francis Zambon. By kind permission Sony / ATV Music Publishing ©
1969. Lyric of *Money (That's What I Want)*. Words and music by Berry
Gordy and Janie Bradford © 1958, Jobete Music Co. Inc. / Stone Agate
Music, USA. Reproduced by permission of Jobete Music Co. Inc. / EMI
Music Publishing Ltd, London WC2H 0QY. Reproduced by permission
of International Music Publications Ltd. All rights reserved. Extracts
from www.princes-trust.org/involvedframes.htm, reprinted by
permission of The Prince's Trust. Extract from 'Best of Times, Worst of
Times: Bill Wyman' by Danny Danziger from *The Times* Magazine
30.04.00, copyright © Times Newspaper Ltd 2000, reprinted by
permission of News International Syndication. Lyric of *Don't Worry,
Be Happy*. Words and music by Bobby McFerrin © BMG Music
Publishing Ltd. All rights reserved. Used by permission. Extract from

'101 Ways To Slow Down', copyright © The Guardian 2001, from *The
Guardian* 09.09.01, reprinted by permission of Guardian Newspapers
Limited. Extract from *Billy Elliot* by Melvin Burgess. Screenplay by Lee
Hall (The Chicken House, 2001), Text copyright © Melvin Burgess
2001. Original screenplay by Lee Hall © Universal Studios Publishing
Rights, a division of Universal Studios Licensing Inc., 2001, reprinted
by permission of the publisher. All rights reserved. Extract from 'Why
I Bought My Child A Gun' by Phil Hogan, copyright © The Guardian
2001, from *The Guardian* 04.07.01, reprinted by permission of
Guardian Newspapers Ltd. Extract from '104 Things To Do With A
Banana' by Wayne M. Hilburn from www.dmgi.com/bananas.html,
reprinted by permission of the author. Extract from 'Slip Sliding
Away' by Sophie Radice, copyright © Sophie Radice 2001, from *The
Guardian Weekend* 03.11.01, reprinted by permission of Guardian
Newspapers Ltd. Extract from 'Balloon Buddies' *The Daily Mail*
28.06.01, reprinted by permission of Atlantic Syndication Partners.
Extract from *The Lost Continent* by Bill Bryson (Blackswan, a division
of Transworld Publishers, 1999), copyright © Bill Bryson 1989,
reprinted by permission of the publisher. Lyric of *24 Hours From
Tulsa*. Words by Hal David. Music by Burt Bacharach. © 1963 New
Hidden Valley Music Company / Casa David, USA. Universal / MCA
Music Limited, Elsinore House, 77 Fulham Palace Road, London W6
8JA / Windswept Music (London) Ltd, Hope House, 40 St Peter's Road,
London W6 9BD. Used by permission of Music Sales Ltd. All rights
reserved. International copyright secured.
Whilst every effort has been made to trace owners of copyright
material in this book, there may have been some cases when the
publishers have been unable to contact the owners. We should be
grateful to hear from anyone who recognises copyright material and
who is unacknowledged. We shall be pleased to make the necessary
amendments in future editions of the book.

The authors and publishers wish to thank the following for
permission to reproduce their photographs:
Associated Press p73 (tr); Ardea pp102, 105 (t); David Bebber p108
(tr); Big Pictures p31; Bridgeman Art Library p20 (b); Neil Bruce
Motoring Library p112 (t,m); Jenny Cockell p109; Corbis pp10 (tm, b),
13 (tm), 40 (tm), 55 (t), 56 (all); Paul Cousans p108 (tl); Empics p22
(all), 26 (r); Fortean pp100, 107; FPG pp6 (br, tm), 14, 40 (a), 47 (all),
60; Getty Images pp4, 6 (bl, bm), 10 (tl, tr), 12, 13 (bm, t, b), 18
(both), 28 (t, b), 34, 40 (c), 41 (all), 44, 45, 60 (br), 64 (a–c), 65 (all),
69, 71 (all), 78 (all), 82 (both), 83, 85, 95, 99, 100, 101, 102 (a, b, c, d,
f), 103 (all), 108 (mr, bl), 110 (both), 114, 119, 125, 127 (m, r); Greg
Evans Picture Library pp112 (b); 128 (mr, r); Hulton Getty p21; Image
State p6 (tl), 9 (b), 124 (a); Vaughan Jones pp5 (t); Alberto Korda
Guerillero Heroico (*Che Guevara*) © ADAGP Paris and DACS London
2002 courtesy of Couturier Gallery LA p74; Magnum p94; Desmond
O'Sullivan p104; PA News pp5 (b), 37 (r), 58; Photodisc pp26, 50, 99;
Pictor International pp6 (tr), 38 (both); Popperfoto p70; Powerstock
pp64 (t), 75; Redferns p43; Retna pp9 (tr), 46, 73 (br), 67; Ronald
Grant Archive p30; Rex Features Ltd pp16 (all), 20 (tr, tm, bm, br), 37
(ml), 73 (l), 77, 86, 117, 118, 127 (l); Science Photo Library p111; Louis
Stettner *Promenade Brooklyn 1954* © ADAGP, Paris and DACS London
2002 courtesy of Gallery 292 / Howard Greenberg Gallery p68;
Topham Picturepoint p37 (mr); Universal Pictorial Press pp37 (l).

Commissioned photographs by Haddon Davies pp26 (Pauline Perkins),
48 (Ozone), 49 (Matt McKay), 97 (food stuffs).
The publishers wish to thank Lou Wright.

Cartoons on p85 produced with permission from Tony Husband; pp7,
25, 84 with permission from *Private Eye*; pp8, 61 with permission
from *The Spectator*, pp27, 79, 113 with permission from
Cartoonstock; p86 with permission from *Business Life*; p72 with
permission from *Punch*.

Printed and bound in China
2007
10 9 8 7 6 5 4